STAYING POWER

STAYING POWER

ENCOURAGEMENT FOR PASTORS TO PERSEVERE

CRAIG BRIAN LARSON

BakerBooks
Grand Rapids, Michigan

© 1998 by Craig Brian Larson

Published by Baker Books
a division of Baker Publishing Group
P.O. Box 6287, Grand Rapids, MI 49516-6287
www.bakerbooks.com

Paperback edition published 2005
ISBN 0-8010-9179-9

Previously published as *Pastoral Grit: The Strength to Stand and to Stay* in 1998 by
Bethany House Publishers

Printed in the United States of America

The Library of Congress has cataloged the hardcover edition as follows:

Larson, Craig Brian.
    Pastoral grit : the strength to stand and to stay / by Craig Brian Larson.
        p.   cm. — (Pastor's soul)
    ISBN 1-55661-969-3 (pbk.)
    1. Pastoral theology. 2. Larson, Craig Brian. I. Title. II. Series: Pastor's
soul series.
BV4011.L39   1997
253'.2—dc21   97–45441

Scripture is taken from the HOLY BIBLE, NEW INTERNATIONAL VERSION®.
NIV®. Copyright © 1973, 1978, 1984 by International Bible Society. Used by
permission of Zondervan. All rights reserved.

Craig Brian Larson is editor of PreachingToday.com and Preaching Today audio, pastor of Lake Shore Church in Chicago, Illinois, and coauthor of *Preaching That Connects* (Zondervan, 1994).

CONTENTS

INTRODUCTION

I AM OVERQUALIFIED TO WRITE this book. Not because I have more pastoral grit than others but because I suspect I have felt like giving up more often than most. Thankfully, though, I have rarely succumbed to that impulse. One reason I have not is because of a simple, unshakable conviction that has developed in my soul: Perseverance is central to spiritual life and ministry. Perseverance is the answer when there are no answers (a situation I often confront). Motivational sayings trumpet the need for perseverance, but even the most eloquent can only understate its importance.

When David Goetz of LEADERSHIP proposed I write this book, he gave me this initial assignment: "Name twelve things that make pastors want to quit." That was not hard to do. I've taken my share of lumps since embarking on this calling in 1975. I faxed a list to Dave that has become the twelve chapters that follow.

This book is about ministry—not just perseverance—because in each chapter I explore the root issues of pastoral discouragement and how I have worked through them. Consequently, I think this resource will be useful for readers who struggle as I have, as well as for those who have not faced thoughts of quitting.

For me, at least, the lessons learned have made a huge difference. Earlier in my ministry the desire to give up frequently entered my mind and heart. Currently I can say, in all honesty, that desire is extremely rare.

To write a book about my soul is to recognize the complexity of my emotions and beliefs. As I wrote and rewrote, I discovered something: in the first draft it was difficult to find the truth. I wrote what I thought was true but then realized I had exaggerated, understated, or missed the mark entirely. I wrote what I thought others would expect to hear and then realized I believed otherwise. The more I rewrote, however, the closer to the truth I came.

Even as I review chapters written months apart, I see inconsistencies. I have not reconciled them all, for they represent the process of growth as well as the impossibility of fully knowing oneself. My goal has been to be as honest with myself and with you as I can be, recognizing that to look into myself is indeed to look into a glass darkly.

Obviously what follows are not definitive answers on ministry but rather what I have experienced and learned. Experience is both a great and terrible teacher. From it we learn what is tried and true. From experience we also learn about overreactions to pain.

Where we connect, I pray God's grace will be released into your life, enabling you to serve Christ better. When I am wrong, or not on your wavelength, I ask your forbearance. When a chapter is too dark, please know that in general I am a positive person committed to faith and hope, and I passionately love pastoral ministry and the church of Jesus Christ.

My deep thanks to my editor, David Goetz, for entrusting me with the opportunity to serve others in this way. The great confidence I have in him is one thing that gave me the boldness to write.

My gratitude also goes to Kevin Miller, Ed Rowell, Mark Galli, Rich Doebler, and Marshall Shelley—great friends with whom I have been privileged to partner in ministry through LEADERSHIP over the years. They have taught me numberless things about writing, ministry, and life in Christ, and have significantly influenced who I am.

The longer I am in ministry the more I appreciate the ministry communities of which I have been a part. The two the Lord has used most profoundly in my life have been Christianity Today, Inc. and the Assemblies of God. My thanks to the leaders past and present of these groups. Both have left a deep and beneficial imprint upon the soul you will read about in this book.

My final gratitude goes to my wife, Nancy, and to our sons, Aaron, Ben, Mark, and Brian David. My choices in ministry have always had steep consequences for them and they, too, have persevered. For their sacrifices, may the kingdom fruit of this book be reckoned also to them.

1

INDEXED BY SIZE

IN 1978, AFTER THREE YEARS as a college and youth pastor, I moved with my wife and son to the Chicago suburb of Evanston to plant a church. I was twenty-four and bristling with ambition. Riding the wave of the Jesus revival, the college group I had helped lead had grown to eighty. I heard reports of Illinois churches growing rapidly, and I revered their pastors as role models. I dreamed of planting a church in Evanston that would grow to number in the hundreds.

We started with only three people—myself, my wife, and our two-year-old son—but I had faith and a plan. I would distribute literature door to door in a several-block area and then telephone each of those families the same night.

We moved into our second-floor apartment on Washington Street, and I started working the neighborhood. After slowly developing a list of twenty or so interested people, I tried to launch meetings at the local Holiday Inn, but only a handful came and those never returned.

I kept working my plan but I was never able to pull together even a regular Bible study. As a church planter I was a spectacular bust.

In Evanston I started asking the questions that I would repeat many times in the years to come. Why does God "bless" some pastors and churches and not me? Why won't God answer my prayers? What is it that some people don't like about me? What's the matter with me?

I learned in Evanston that God is not concerned about stroking my ego, which definitely took a beating. There I felt the full effect of what it means to index my identity to the size of my church. Of course I had done that when leading the college group, but I had always had "success" before. Now the equation worked against me and it hurt badly.

I played baseball for several years in grade school. Only once did I pitch. On that fateful day the manager summoned me to the mound after several other pitchers had taken their lumps. Well, I changed that; I did not take any lumps because I did not give anyone a chance to swing. I threw one ball after another, walking the batters, loading the bases. Then I walked in run after run.

When you are failing on the mound, that spot in the center of the field is a stark, lonely hill. You hear teammates and coaches and parents yelling, "You can do it!" "Just get it over the plate!" "Make him hit it!" You feel as though everyone in creation is witnessing your inability to produce, and you groan inside as you fail them— one pitch at a time.

I do not recall if I started crying out there on the mound but I know I felt like it. I died several dozen deaths that day, my male ego mortally wounded each time my pitch hit the catcher's glove or kicked up a little pile of dust somewhere around home plate and skidded in futility to the back fence; each time that umpire yelled out for all to hear how I had missed the mark. It was perhaps the most devastating day in my young athletic life. Finally, after far too long, my coach walked to the mound and mercifully took away the baseball.

That day is the closest thing I know to what it is like to pastor a church that will not go. Heaven and earth, it seems, look to you to carry the day, and the day just will not budge. You feel like a fool—a failure who is letting others down. (Perhaps the most ludicrous part of it all is when denominational superiors or well-meaning others try to say things to motivate you to get your church to grow, as if you are not motivated and are not trying!)

I guess there is another analogy for what it feels like to pastor a shrinking church, or one that has plateaued. I have had my share of dreams in which I am in public or, worse yet, in a church meeting, and for some unexplainable reason I am there in the buff. The shame in these dreams is overwhelming. Proverbs 14:28 says, "A large population is a king's glory, but without subjects a prince is ruined." When I stand as pastor to a group of thirty people, I can feel naked. Leaders by definition have followers, and those who don't are not leaders, or so you think. False shame—not hardship or little money—is really what grinds pastors of smaller churches to dust, to despair, to a desire to quit.

After one year in Evanston I desired precisely that. Explain it as best I could—"I feel led to another place";

"It just doesn't seem God is in this"—the truth was, I was discouraged and nothing was going right and I did not know what else to do. I asked my superintendent to come out to the mound and put me out of my misery.

Into the fire

I told my superintendent I felt called to inner-city ministry, so he recommended me to a church several blocks from Comiskey Park on the south side of Chicago. The church had twenty-five saints in a small building, across the street from a block-square government housing project. Most people in the church were poor, and the church was poor, but I was determined to be their full-time pastor.

The first year a few trickled away and none replaced them. To an ever-increasing degree, much more was at stake in the numbers than my ego. This was stark survival in a hostile environment. This was visceral desperation.

I felt like a green insurance salesman on full commission. Such salesmen do not have the luxury of worrying about their ego; they watch the numbers in terms of feeding the children. Frankly, I watched our attendance less for my compassion for people who needed Christ and more for my livelihood.

But there in the wasteland, God and I developed something special in our relationship, and there he taught me how he would work through me, as he works through each of us uniquely. This Judean desert was one of the defining periods of my life and the one that gave me the greatest hope, for after one year of slow decline we turned a corner. We held a week-long outreach that brought life, hope, and even a few souls into the congregation. That started seven years of slow, incremental growth. Each year five or ten new people would take a liking to us; a precious few would decide to follow Christ, be baptized, become members. Gradually the church grew stronger in community, leadership, and maturity. When I left the church after eight and a half years, we averaged around ninety on Sunday mornings.

At this church I learned that, for me at least, numbers take time. My mix of assets, gifts, and passions do not add up to quick results. On the natural level, my voice, personality, and appearance are not commanding. As a leader I am a consensus builder who patiently lays the groundwork of vision and values rather than a mover and a shaker. As an evangelist I work at leading others to Christ but I see few conversions. My primary gifting is teaching and preaching.

Even so, I know God uses me. Time is on my side because God has a purpose for me and he wants to build his church. If I just hang in there with prayer, faith, and diligence, doing well what I do best—time is surely on my side.

I am convinced by verses such as John 15:8 that God wants to bring fruitfulness of some sort (not necessarily significant church growth) from each of us, but we cannot put a deadline on it. The fruit may take a year, three years, thirty years. But if I am spiritually vital, if I work hard and pray with faith, sooner or later God will build his church.

That conviction requires several things of me. I must have patience. I cannot be intimidated by the expectations of others but must have a sense of security about who God has made me. And I must have faith in God's Word despite what I see now. In short, I must follow in the steps of Abraham.

No other person shows how important it is to give God time. In Abraham, God did many of his greatest works over a long span of time. Abraham did not even embark on his greatest adventure with God until he was seventy-five, and it was another twenty-five before Isaac brought laughter to his tent. Abraham's descendants did not inherit the Promised Land until hundreds of years after his death, and the full measure of God's promise to give Abraham descendants like the sand by the seashore is still being fulfilled thousands of years later. From Abraham I learn that when I give God time, he does a work greater in breadth and scope than I can imagine.

God has an interesting perspective on my life—eternity—and he has a way of working with that perspective in mind. The One who knows the end from the beginning never feels rushed, knowing full well that many of his highest purposes are fulfilled through what is my greatest frustration: time.

My experience of pastoring near Comiskey Park developed these convictions like cement footings in my soul. Then I moved northwest thirty miles to suburban Arlington Heights and a church of thirty people that met in a grade school gym. In this upscale suburb my convictions were tested, found true, then tested in another way.

Arlington lows

In Arlington Heights I would pastor three years. The first year went as my first year in Chicago had: seemingly nothing happened. Even though I was armed with my convictions about perseverance, this year was nevertheless equally hard for me because I was now much more driven by numbers than before. My drivenness had many sources:

- I thought I was in my prime, that this was an area conducive to church growth, and that God had clearly led me to this church with "blessing" in mind.
- I dearly wanted to be respected by my peers. In retrospect I think this was my primary motivation. (Lord, have mercy.)
- I wanted to see people come to Christ, be helped, and grow in full devotion to Christ.
- I wanted to be a part of a strong, fruitful, dynamic community of believers.
- I wanted to survive financially, not only as a church but as a full-time pastor with a family of five (soon to be six). We were again in a pioneer situation, with a large neighboring church committed to support the church $400 a month for one year, and then we would be on our own, do or die.
- I wanted to produce so this supporting church would feel their investment was worthwhile.
- I wanted to make our church more attractive to visitors. One of the high hurdles for smaller churches is that many newcomers want to attend a larger church (but your church cannot expand until they attend).

Valid perception or not, I had the sense that our size was an automatic limitation, preventing us from reaching people.

- I wanted to bolster my identity. I still felt as though being the pastor of a small church meant I was insignificant.
- I believed that what I read in church-growth literature could happen for me.
- I wanted to be respected by my denominational superiors.

A large batch of mixed motives, to be sure, which brought mixed results. After one year at Arlington Heights we turned a corner. Although few visitors had previously ventured into our grade school gym, one Sunday in January our attendance nearly doubled—and most of those newcomers joined the congregation. As the spring progressed, we added more people, with attendances climbing into the eighties. This fed my appetite for growth, an appetite that had big downsides. Aside from my mixed motives being displeasing to the Lord, the more driven I became for numbers the more prone I was to despair.

I grew discouraged more easily because my emotions were linked to attendance rather than to individual growth in Christ. An "up" Sunday caused me to dream euphorically of greater things. A down day left me despairing that all was lost. Every visitor brought promise; every discontented member threatened my dream. Emotionally I was subject to others and to circumstances instead of being directed from within by my identity in

God. No worse roller coaster exists than the one I rode when my emotions were tied to Sunday attendance.

A pastor friend recently admitted to those of us at a pastors' meeting that for some six years he had ministered with the wrong motives. "I was doing ministry 'in the flesh,'" he said. "I was using people. Flesh gives birth to flesh; only Spirit gives birth to Spirit. So I was dead; they were dead. By the time I got up to preach each Sunday, I was completely discouraged by thinking about those who weren't there, and I was ready to quit every single week.

"Then last summer God spoke to me about my motivations. He showed me my heart and it wasn't pretty. He asked me if I was willing to serve him even if we never grew. I had to admit that I wasn't willing, that I was serving numbers not God. But God broke me. I dedicated myself to setting my heart on God not growth, and it has made all the difference in the world in my attitude and in my ability to lead this church."

Another fallout from my mixed motives was that I became somewhat manipulative and angry. Yes, angry. That has been one of my biggest surprises, in retrospect, to realize that during this time I was an angry person, though others probably did not see it. The more driven I was for numbers, the more disappointed I became with those who were not performing the way I wanted them to and were thereby frustrating my dreams. The more frustrated I became with people, the less I enjoyed my ministry. The more I tried to administrate and "make things happen," the more discouraged I became when I could not.

I found out firsthand that God and people control church growth; I do not. If God and others did not do what I wanted when I wanted it, my emotions were subject to meltdown. Too much of my energy was tied up in something I could influence but not control. With church attendance, too much was at stake for me personally: my very identity, my future, my hopes. The temptation to try to manipulate God and others becomes overwhelming, and that is a prescription for anger and failure.

I have heard that anger leads to depression, and from my own experience I think it is true. It seems to be true for others as well. A friend of mine has a relative who went to Bible school and then became a pastor. He was sharp and highly motivated. He read books on church growth, management, leadership, and success. He went to seminars for pastors. His goal was growth, and his church grew—but not fast enough for him. Even though his church was fruitful and filled with potential, he was in deep despair. After a few years he resigned from the church, quit the ministry, and went into business.

An excessive focus on numbers as an end in itself leads to discouragement for another reason. I tended to compare myself and our church with others. I could not hear what was happening in another church without comparing it with what was happening in our church, and ours almost never measured up. My expectations were higher than God's. Comparing myself with others was completely unrealistic.

After two years in Arlington Heights, my bubble burst. A small group of people rose in opposition to my leadership and talked to others in the congregation about how they felt. Within a few months the church dropped in attendance by nearly half. We were back to square one; and those who left were the workers.

That revolt was the first large-scale opposition I had ever faced in ministry. But it proved to be a gift from God, for it taught me how vulnerable the size of a church is. Basing my identity on numbers was like building my life on soap bubbles. Abraham Lincoln once said: It is foolish to take either praise or criticism too seriously. The same goes for church attendance. The numbers on Sunday are not *who I am*. My true identity is who I am in God.

The LEADERSHIP *years*

It took a five-year hiatus from pastoring, however, for this truth to settle thoroughly into my soul. I stayed at Arlington Heights for nearly a year after the meltdown, and then Marshall Shelley at LEADERSHIP invited me to work as an associate editor.

There my eyes were opened to what had happened to me (rather, what I had done to myself) while pastoring. For the first time in twelve years, my identity was connected to something other than the size of my church. New acquaintances no longer asked how big my church was as their first question. For my soul, it was as striking a change as moving to another country or another planet as the reference points of my self-concept were realigned. An emotional block of limestone had been lifted from my shoulders.

What magnified my new realization further was my conversations with pastors. With somewhat of an outsider's perspective (I was still credentialed and continued to preach), I saw them going through the same syndrome I had experienced. When I asked about their churches, most answered first in terms of numbers, and no matter what the size of their church, they usually did so apologetically. I wanted to say, "You do not have to apologize! I am not taking your measure by how big your church is!"

But in my case, the fault was not in other people or in pastoring as a role, but in allowing myself to subscribe to a false value system. To measure a church primarily by its size is to miss how Christ evaluates a church. In Revelation, when Jesus wrote to the seven churches, he addressed issues of *quality* not quantity. I had let myself be controlled by the expectations of others. I was seeking to please people rather than God.

I learned something else during this hiatus: No one can minister to everyone. Each of us is wired by God in such a way that no matter how godly or gifted we are at ministry, we will be able to minister only to certain people effectively. Our vision and values, personality and gifts will touch some and not others. I must not take personally another person's decision not to attend our church. They may choose not to attend because they don't like the color of our walls, or our music, or any number of reasons. We are going to be able to minister to a certain number of people and win a certain number of people to Christ. I need to be true to how God has made me and let God work through me with whomever he will.

Another molding force in my life was Daniel Brown, pastor of The Coastlands in Aptos, California, who gave me a more realistic perspective on ministry. Brown says we tend to view a church as a reservoir, and so our goal is to accumulate as much in the reservoir as possible. The real point of ministry can become accumulation instead of changing lives. And that is a model for frustration because in our volatile culture people are always leaving.

Better, says Brown, to view church ministry as a river. When people enter the river, we are called to bring the Gospel and discipleship into their lives for as long as they remain in the water. But sooner or later, most move on (how many in your church today were there five years ago?), and with a river paradigm, that is okay because the important thing is what God has put into people's lives while they have been with us. The measure of my ministry is not how wide the river is; it is the degree of growth and fruitfulness that occurs while a person is in our tributary.

To use another model, I look at pastoring believers the way a schoolteacher looks at teaching students. A teacher's goal is not to hold on to as many students as possible for as long as possible, but rather to build as much as possible into students' lives while he or she has them.

Armed with this new perspective on church ministry, in August 1995 I became pastor of a church of thirty-five people, which meets in a high-rise in downtown Chicago. I answered this call with a conscious determination that

I would not fall back into the numbers obsession that had caused me such despair in the past. I would focus on the quality of our ministry in evangelism and discipleship, and trust that quantity was simply a byproduct of obedience to Christ.

The first effect of that determination was that I entered upon this stage of pastoring with more joy than anything I had ever done. On my first Sunday I wanted to tell God over and over again how thankful I was that he had allowed me to pastor.

The second effect was that now, two years into this ministry, I can say that discouragement has been extremely rare.

Of course, my convictions are being tested. So far we have seen growth in individuals and we are progressing well in crystallizing the church's vision and values, but numerically we have stayed steady at around thirty-five on Sunday mornings. We have gained some people and seen others move on.

In three months I will have my annual review with my denominational superior, and I am starting to feel a tinge of anxiety. He has made it clear that he wants to see results, that my ministry will fall short "if you're having good services and people love each other, but in three years the church is still running thirty-five people."

At this meeting I will have to point to progress primarily in intangibles and brace myself to hold true to my convictions. I refuse to be ashamed of the size of our church, for that has proven deadly to me and to the church.

The other thing testing this conviction of late is some

of the comments of people in our church. I sense that some feel insecure about the numbers. They want to grow, as I do. But I think some of them may also be concerned that I will lose heart and leave. I occasionally make comments to reassure them about this. I keep saying that I am in this church for the long haul, Lord willing, and I am convinced that over a period of several decades we will see significant progress.

A few weeks ago a man called me on a Sunday morning and asked about attending our church. Toward the end of the conversation, he asked how large our church was. After I told him, he said, "I was looking for a larger church. Can you recommend one in your area?"

I gave him the phone number of the largest church in the city, and he said good-bye. I put down the phone and realized something wonderful. I was not the least bit resentful, insecure, or discouraged about what he had said. I smiled at the thought, picked up my Bible, and went with enthusiasm and confidence to minister to those whom God would bring our way that day.

I was free.

2

DIGGING OUT OF MY FINANCIAL WINTER

THE WINTER OF 1979 took a chunk out of my soul. My wife, two sons, and I were living in the Chicago suburb of Evanston where I was attempting to pioneer a church from scratch. On New Years Eve several feet of snow fell; for a day or two the streets were impassable. We lived in an apartment with no garage and parked our '73 Plymouth Fury on the street. The snowplows finally came through, but they piled a high ridge of snow against the cars parked along the curb. I had to shovel for two hours to get my car out.

But that was only the beginning. When I returned from my errand to the grocery store, someone else had pulled into the spot I had cleared and I had to shovel to get my car into another unplowed space. For three months, almost every time I came or went in my car, I had to shovel more snow. The already limited street parking became even more scarce, and I would often have to park several blocks from our apartment.

And the snow kept falling. It came in wave upon wave, interspersed with subzero blasts of arctic air. It seemed winter would never end. Of course through all this I was trying to pioneer a church by canvassing door to door. For two months I could do precious little of that, and my church-planting effort ended in futility. I have never forgotten how bad weather can complicate what you are trying to do.

Money pressures can be like that. For much of my twenty-two years in ministry my financial situation has resembled a Chicago winter. Usually I try to ignore the weather, but even then it influences my mood and my activities. As much as I have tried to ignore money, it influences everything: when I have enough, my life feels like a crisp autumn day filled with sunshine; when I don't, it is like a cold front hammering down from Canada's Hudson Bay.

For most of these twenty-two years my personal finances have been difficult, sometimes desperately so. In my first year as a pastor in Chicago, my income was around $14,000. Over the next eight years the church gradually increased my salary. When I left it was somewhere around $25,000. Throughout this time my wife did not work outside our home.

Our possessions reflected our situation. In Chicago we drove a rusty 1974 Chevy Malibu. The rubber door seals had become corroded, and when it rained, several inches of water collected in the floor well of the rear seats. I stuffed newspapers through the trunk into the rusted-out tire wells to keep water and debris out.

We lived in a second-floor, two-bedroom apartment, and when the wind blew from the south, the astringent fumes from a factory were almost unbearable. The building's old windows rattled in the winter breeze and the drafts were terrible. I became proficient at catching mice (peanut butter is better bait than cheese), adding "trapper" to the many pastoral hats I wore. I felt locked in by our penury. We never had any savings, and it was all we could do to keep up with quarterly tax payments.

When we moved to Arlington Heights, I received roughly the same salary, but we lived in an area with a higher cost of living. On one occasion after our church's annual business meeting, in which annual expenses are reported—including my salary—a church member said to me, "I didn't know it was possible to live in this area on less than $30,000. How do you do it?"

Not very well. Nothing has made ministry harder for me than financial pressure. Nothing gives me a greater feeling of "I can't go on." I recall a few times of such despair and desperation that—despite my love for pastoral ministry—I was willing to do any kind of work just to pay my bills and be out from under the pressure. I even fleetingly thought about buying a lottery ticket.

I see now that my financial woes have not solely been the result of a slim salary. I see rather that my financial winters have been my responsibility, a confluence of two streams: my personal weaknesses and my personal convictions.

Anti-control freak

We have done a few things right with our money: we have been good givers and we have largely avoided debt.

I learned both virtues in my home church. My pastor gave unselfishly and he taught us to do the same. But the church also constructed a new building that soared over budget, and for the next decade and more the resulting debt was a galactic black hole that consumed time, attention, energy, pastors, money—seemingly everything. That experience has defined my attitude toward debt. Even in the case of serious needs, my family and I have generally gone without rather than charge it—and that has been our financial salvation.

My weakness, however, is a failure to budget. Several times I have worked up a budget plan, but it has always broken down at the point of recording expenditures. So for twenty-two years we have followed the cash-flow method of budgeting: buy only what we need, and when the cash stops flowing, we stop buying.

That method has one huge drawback. It fails to prepare you for large expenditures, emergency or non-emergency. Consequently we have had scarce wardrobes, no savings, no home of our own, a thirteen-year-old car, and a host of ancient appliances. (I have repaired our portable dishwasher so often—bought a year after our marriage—that it looks like it tumbled down a mountainside.) Emergencies have been just that.

For the longest time I rationalized that we didn't budget because we had no discretionary funds. Every penny we spent was for real needs, not wants. But even though our income has slowly increased over the years, we have yet to successfully develop a budget.

I think the true culprit is the fact that I don't like to organize and control things—or people. Administration keeps me from what I love. I am an idea person, a word person, a thinker more than a doer. I constantly analyze, question, read, explain, and try to understand. I love to organize ideas, but not money or files. Furthermore, I love to seek the Lord's face in the spiritual disciplines of Bible reading and prayer. I have to consciously *limit* myself or that is all I would do. Gradually I have learned to administrate and organize out of necessity and a desire to be a faithful steward, but these duties I keep to the bare minimum.

Two myths

In junior high I walked a half mile to school. During winter that took a toll on my hands. They would become severely chapped until they cracked and bled. My mother pleaded with me to use lotion, but despite my pain I largely ignored her admonition. After all, in a few months spring would come and my hands would get better.

For about the first five years of my ministry, I had a similarly childlike approach to my personal finances. I simply ignored the pain and bleeding as much as possible, keeping my eyes on my work. Two myths encouraged me to do this:

1. *We cannot live on what we make.* This was perhaps the most destructive myth because it caused me to give up hope of gradually working toward financial strength through sound principles. Instead, I put all my hope in God to miraculously turn our circumstances around. Of course he can do that, but normally he has another agenda: to mold us through the struggle to learn self-control, wisdom, and planning skills.

The truth is, I can live within my means whatever my income level. Many "needs" are determined by the standards I set and the choices I make. From cars to food, I often assume I must have a certain level of quality or comfort that has little to do with my true needs. I sometimes wonder what Elijah or Paul or Christian workers in places like China would think of my "lean" living. The realization that I can live within my means if I work hard at it gives me hope and strength.

2. Ministers are underpaid. This myth depends on my measuring stick. I can use a human standard and say pastors should earn what teachers or CEOs or the general middle-class public make, but where do I find that in Scripture? Furthermore, recent research shows the trend is toward better pay for pastors. The myth that all pastors are underpaid only made me feel sorry for myself and be occasionally resentful toward church people, perhaps even toward the Lord. Instead of working hard to live decently on what we had, perhaps I wanted to suffer in order to spite those who paid our salary. Martyrdom can be great revenge.

Unlike the season that ravaged my hands, our finances faced a long-term winter, and ignoring them only made things worse. I finally decided that while personal financial management took me away from things I considered more spiritual, God must have wanted me to spend some time at it. Despite our faithful tithing, he did not unleash a flood of money to wash away our problems the easy way. We have had to learn how to manage things. God does provide in extraordinary ways at times, but usually he wants to work through our wisdom and hard work.

That lesson was reinforced by what I saw in Genesis 39 about Joseph, whom God singularly blessed. Joseph was a crack manager. As Jesus taught, he who is faithful with a few things will be given charge over more.

We need to major in our strengths. If we put too much time into our weaknesses, so the logic goes, we will dissipate our strengths. I have taken consolation from this concept, but I have also used it to rationalize a lack of growth and make it easy to bail out on a difficult task. If you stretch a large sail to the wind but the hull has a gaping hole in it, the boat will sink. In other words, if I lack those around me to whom I can delegate what I do not excel in, I must maintain a minimum of competence in those areas in order to make the most of my strengths.

How I handle my money becomes a spiritual issue. Money management can lead to spiritual growth. God wants me involved.

Guided by convictions

Mixed with this muddy stream of my weaknesses, several key convictions have guided my financial habits. Some I held simplistically; I have had to nuance them because they helped me rationalize my weaknesses. Others were sound, but I did not anticipate their real-world repercussions.

My wife should not work outside the home. My wife and

I had four boys over the course of thirteen years. We decided together that she should stay home while they were young and not work outside the home. At first, our conviction was based on Scripture, then it simply became our preference. In an economy geared toward two-income families, our choice obviously allotted us smaller margins to work with.

I would love to be able to say that God rewards families in which the mother stays home—that they will do as well as if she worked outside the home—but that has not been our experience. When our youngest son went to school a few years ago, Nancy started working part-time, and it has helped us significantly. Certainly our boys are better off for our decision that Nancy stay home with them, and I am glad we did it that way. What I should have realized at the time, however, is the message of Scripture that tells us convictions often entail sacrifice.

Money should never determine location of ministry. I want to follow God's call no matter the size of the church or the salary. Ministry should not be a climb up the career and paycheck ladder. That attitude, however, may have kept me from making my true needs known to the church leaders who decided my compensation. Over the years I have learned what I hope is a healthy mixture of faith and realism. I need to be willing to step out in faith, but I also need to communicate what I require to support my family and then prayerfully leave the final decision with the Lord and the decision makers.

Before coming to my current position, for example, I felt strongly that God was directing me to this church, but I was determined to tell the leaders what I needed to adequately support my family. The amount sounded exorbitant, but I felt it was the right thing to do. As it turned out, my salary request exceeded what they had planned to pay by about 50 percent, but they accepted my request without dissent. If I had asked for less, that is what I would have gotten, and would be living with the repercussions.

If I seek first God's kingdom and righteousness, I will not have to concern myself with money. That, of course, is not exactly what Jesus said. He never suggests that I am to be a passive recipient of God's provision. Rather, the weight of Scripture is that God normally uses me in the process, and that means I will have to give money some serious thought.

Occasionally such thought involved decisions that felt self-serving to me. After a poor offering at our first church in Chicago, for example, I sometimes had to decide between the church paying my salary or the utilities. I had heard other pastors say that under such circumstances the church bills should be paid first. But after trying that I decided it did the church no good to force my family and me to sooner or later find another church because we could not afford to stay. The church had a responsibility to pay its worker his due. So I took out my salary, and the church utilities always found a way of getting paid. If I always made myself the fall guy for church problems, I stood in the way of God's promise.

Money is hazardous material. More often than not the

New Testament warns of the spiritual dangers of mammon. For that reason, outside of paying my current bills, I have never had a desire to pile up money.

Still, deep in the catacombs of my heart, I think some other motivation may be at work. I have never owned a home and currently rent a three-bedroom duplex, though we could have purchased it if we had wanted to. The truth is, I feel more spiritual when I am relatively poor, and that may be a sign of some sort of distortion in my spirituality. Am I trying to impress God or earn his favor by doing without?

In ministry I must be willing to suffer for Christ. I have, and I have not always liked it. In general, though, I have withstood hardship and felt honored to do without for Christ's sake. That blinded me, however, to what hardship did to my family. I thought they should be just as happy to endure hardship as I was. But we were in a place that I chose to be. The person who makes such a choice has a much easier time of it than those who follow along.

I learned this the hard way. On one occasion, my teenage son and I had a heated argument—unusual for us—and he said to me, "What kind of a man are you? You can't even provide for your family!"

That got my attention. Although the rest of the world judges a man by how much money he makes, in my naïveté it had never occurred to me that someone in my own family might judge me by that standard.

Actually money was not the real problem, for leanness does not in itself cause resentment. But I didn't take the time to do enough of the fun family things that were within our means. I was focused on the church, loved to work, and was content. Having fun was not one of my higher priorities. In addition, I may have been guilty of poor mouthing—too often saying no to something the kids wanted, stating the reason to be a lack of funds.

Courage for the promised land

I have made many mistakes for which I will have to deal with the consequences for some time to come. Yet despite all this God has shown his grace. He has used finances like a spiritual ballast in my life—stabilizing me by forcing me to deal with distortions in my thinking. God has met our needs without fail and blessed us with excellent health. In our financially vulnerable state, he has protected us from the large financial crises that would have created a hole from which we could not climb out. My oldest sons, now in college, are extremely hardworking and self-reliant. Through our times of need I have learned to pray more effectively, I've gained faith from seeing God provide, and I have empathy for others in need.

Finally, my wife and I are actually working toward getting on a budget. We have started by recording expenditures for six "critical control zones," such as groceries, on accounting paper taped right into the checkbook. When we get the recording habit down, we plan to set monthly amounts for each category of spending and then stay within the limits.

One "north star" by which I have navigated throughout has been the experience of Abraham and Isaac. Genesis 12 says God appeared to Abraham, commanded him to move to the land of Canaan, and gave him extravagant promises. Abraham obeyed, enduring the hardship of moving hundreds of miles away, and when he came to the place he was specifically told to go—the land of promise—he found something unexpected: famine.

That was hard not only on Abraham but on the hundreds who lived with him. Imagine hearing the cries of the children in his camp for food and water. Imagine facing the questions and doubts of Sarah, Lot, and the others in his company. The famine was so severe Abraham felt he must move south to Egypt to survive.

Isaac, too, experienced famine in the Promised Land, according to Genesis 26. Like his father, Isaac considered moving to Egypt, but God appeared to him and said, "Do not go down to Egypt; live in the land where I tell you to live. Stay in this land for a while, and I will be with you and will bless you." In faith and obedience, Isaac stayed put. Eventually God blessed him for it, giving him a hundredfold harvest from the seed he planted.

I have received that as a promise and a paradigm for my life. For a time, the "promised land" can be a hostile place. But sooner or later, if I persevere—faithfully doing my part and accepting my financial responsibilities— God will fulfill his purposes for me and bring about a great harvest of the sort he desires.

The place to which God calls me is not easy to possess, especially in the initial stages. It takes time (hundreds of years for Abraham and his descendants). It takes courage and faith (too often I have wanted a situation that requires no faith at all). It takes a willingness to endure famine and live in tents like a nomad. But I believe the glory that will eventually be revealed in this life and immeasurably more in the age to come will make this hardship seem trifling by comparison. The promised land may not always be the easiest place to be, but it is my spiritual home.

3

LIGHT FROM AN EIGHT-WATT MINISTRY

IN GRADE SCHOOL I played the saxophone for two years and then quit. One event that no doubt contributed to this was the annual concert held at the junior high school across town. I remember only one song from that concert: "Red River Valley." And although I liked the song before the concert, I do not recall it fondly. On that evening I sat in front of more people than I ever had in my memory: a sea of students' parents, brothers and sisters, aunts and uncles.

We came to the end of "Red River Valley," and we were supposed to play it twice. So I plowed ahead, blew hard, and belted out the first note of the song. But my plaintive G was the only sound that came forth from the orchestra. Somehow—I still do not know how—everyone else knew we were playing the song only once. Even though I stopped after one note, that one honk was enough. The crowd laughed, all the kids in the orchestra turned and looked at me, and I turned as red as the river.

I have blown my share of wrong notes in ministry as well. I do not like to do things poorly. When I feel unqualified—whether by talent or temperament—I am tempted to quit while I am behind.

Each year my denomination asks pastors to file a report on what is happening numerically in our churches. A few times I have been proud to complete it, but in general I dislike the report because the hard numbers reveal a weakness in me. My pastoral ministry has not borne a significant number of conversions. This is not because I lack desire. I want to lead others to Christ. I work at relational evangelism. In public I include salt in my conversations. In church I preach a number of evangelistic sermons each year and include a gospel component in many others. I ask for a response after I preach, but the fruit simply is not there.

I can beat myself up pretty good over this. In times of discouragement in my first three pastorates, I told myself someone else could reach our neighborhood much better than I could; I should resign so that a more evangelistic pastor could get the job done. Too often I have dragged myself over the hot coals for my personality. *I am too reserved*, I tell myself. *I do not have a magnetic personality.* And on it goes. In a few seasons of my ministry, I rehearsed a virtual catalog of why I cannot pastor, and I would be as familiar with it as with anything in the Bible.

When I feel unqualified for my task, I easily rationalize quitting. I argue that I would be doing God, the church, and the world a favor. *I am in the way, Lord. Look how I botched up that last service. I did not plan well and during announcements I had to ask someone in the congregation for some information. The musician did not know when to come forward, and I did not forewarn the pianist about a song I wanted to sing after the sermon. In sum, I am the wrong man for the job.*

Of course, this line is as old as the burning bush. I have preached about the reluctant Moses, the depressed Elijah, the "aw, shucks" Gideon, and sincerely uttered the clichés: "God does not look for ability, he looks for . . ."

Nevertheless, when I feel like I'm flunking, I know what it's like to want to drop out.

Character, not ability

At such a time, I deceive myself into thinking the issue is ability or personality rather than my character. But nobody really flunks out of high school; they drop out.

On the surface, my desire to quit because I am unqualified appears to come from a low opinion of myself, but, in fact, it betrays a healthy streak of pride. I want to appear better than I am to conceal my weaknesses. I want to airbrush my reputation the way a magazine photographer airbrushes blemishes. When God calls me to a task that reveals my flaws, it threatens my self-inflated image.

I felt this drive to conceal my weakness when I came to my current pastorate. The church of thirty-five could not afford a full-time pastor and had been without one for six months. My presbyter asked me to consider serving as interim pastor, and I accepted the role.

After six months I came to a moment of truth. I felt God's call to become the regular pastor of the church, but I saw the risks. Numerically the congregation hovered tenuously at the thirty-five plateau. As a part-time pastor I had limited time to invest in further activities that would spur growth. The church's principal layleader had already informed me that he was searching for a home in the suburbs and would leave the church when they moved.

I visualized what would happen: the church would keel over into a tailspin. If I became the pastor, I could not walk away from a declining situation in the way that an interim pastor could. I would be stuck with a church failure on my hands—not something I wanted to be associated with. My pride told me to back away from a situation that would most likely hurt my reputation, but I was convinced of God's leading. In the end, I overcame my pride and decided to entrust my reputation to him; I assumed the pastorate.

There is a second character issue at stake when I am tempted to quit because I feel unqualified. It is self-pity.

I guess I am in good company. When Elijah fled from Jezebel into the desert, he eventually lay down under a tree and prayed, "I have had enough, Lord. Take my life; I am no better than my ancestors." In Elijah's confession of inadequacy, I do not sense humility but self-pity. Likewise, when I have discounted my ability to finish God's work, I have often felt sorry for myself. *Poor me, I am not as good as other pastors. Poor me, I am going to fail. Poor me, others will think less of me.*

Self-pity provides a perverse satisfaction that can be addictive. The satisfaction comes from passive-aggressive actions against God, my tacit complaint over how he made me. It comes from how self-pity gives me a great excuse for doing nothing. It is hugely self-absorbing. It is so addictive that part of the pathology of self-pity is that it motivates me to kick myself when I am down.

When I am in a normal state of mind, I see the sin and self-destruction of feeling sorry for myself. When my boys have fallen into self-pity over a loss in sports, I have told them, "Never fall into self-pity. It will make you a loser. Once you enjoy feeling sorry for yourself, you will not mind failure." But once again, though I know this, I do not always see the dynamics when they occur in me.

New perspectives

My days of beating up on myself are largely over, and several things account for this.

First, I am learning the mindset needed to work for God.

The summer before my senior year in college, I worked for a house builder. When I started, I already knew the basic skills of carpentry—how to hammer nails and saw wood—but I knew nothing about how to put a house together. I could not read blueprints. I did not know how walls and floors and ceilings connected.

If I had perceived my job as a house builder, I would have quit the first day. But that was not my job. The builder hired me to assist him. He built houses; I followed orders. For the walls, he sawed top and bottom plates and marked every sixteen inches where I was to nail the studs. For the roof, he showed me where to lay sheets of plywood and I nailed them down. Throughout the framing process, he regularly laid his level against walls and floors to check for plumb.

This builder was a tall, thick man who worked with boundless vigor, and I did my best to keep up with him. He was on the job early in the morning, before I arrived, and stayed after I pedaled my bike for home. I did not set the pace, he did. I saw myself as working with a human dynamo.

This is the attitude I am learning in ministry. Instead of taking all the responsibility on my shoulders, I am trying to imitate Christ, who said, "My Father is always at his work to this very day, and I, too, am working" (John 5:17). If Jesus, the Son of God, saw himself in the capacity I was in with the home builder, how much more must I?

Of course, how to work with God is not usually as clear. I cannot see him, and his directions are not always as easy to hear and grasp as the builder's were to me. If I didn't know better, I could get the idea that the work all depended on me! But I am in a mysterious partnership with God, in which he assures me that if I am prayerful and dependent on the Holy Spirit, he will work through me. The work is his business.

Second, I am not as hard on myself anymore because I am more realistic about whom I can reach and when.

In previous stages of my ministry, I believed I should reach everyone. Every visitor should join our church, and if I was a good enough preacher they would. Every person without Christ with whom I shared the Gospel should become a believer that day, and if I were really filled with the Spirit the person would. When people did not return to church or commit themselves to Christ, I took it personally. Any lack of response meant something was wrong with me.

I do not believe that anymore (though I certainly have a lot of growing yet to do). I have learned God has not called me to be everything to everyone. He has designed me with a unique personality, gifting, and background, and who I am in Christ will reach some people extremely well, while others not at all. My inability to minister to some people does not mean I am unqualified for ministry. I may be poorly equipped to reach some, but I am tremendously qualified to reach others.

I have finally come to the place where I am willing to accept this and, with more difficulty, accept the limitations that come with it. For more than a decade of my ministry I looked to other fruitful ministers and figured if I could be more like them and do more like them I would bear more fruit, which was and is my passion.

Besides the inauthentic feel of such imitation, on a pragmatic level it simply did not work. So I have turned over the business of fruit and numbers to God. If through my best efforts, highest faith, and best thinking he gives me fifty people, so be it. If he gives me fifty thousand or the entire city, better yet. I still pursue personal growth and ministry skills, perhaps even obsessively, but I no longer regard myself as inadequate because I cannot reach everyone. If I am spiritually vital, diligent, and filled with faith, God will use me to touch some, and that must be enough.

Naturally I am still tested. Last year a dental student and his wife began attending our church. After several months they started attending less frequently, and so I phoned to see if everything was all right. Spiritually they were doing fine, but I learned something that disheartened me for a while. They had started attending a mid-week home Bible study sponsored by another church—a Korean church, and our dental student is Korean.

I saw the writing on the wall. Even though this couple had frequently expressed their appreciation for my preaching and our church, I thought they would surely gravitate toward the Korean church. I felt competitive. I began thinking about how we could improve our ministry so we would not lose couples like these. But after struggling over this for a week, I finally turned the matter over to the Lord. If the other church was spiritually vital, I gave God "permission" to lead them there if he wanted to; I was not going to take it personally. As it turned out, they have stayed in our church and have become strongly involved.

Another reason I am now able to more quickly get over my tendency to take a "failure" personally is that I have come to see ministry as a process rather than an event. My job is to move people along as far as possible in the direction of God, but if it is not God's time, I do not have to reap the harvest. My calling from God is to plant seeds and do what I can. No matter how well I do my part through the Holy Spirit, many people will not respond.

Jesus himself ministered with this assumption. When he told the rich young ruler to give away his wealth and follow him, the man turned away. Still, Jesus did not chase after him, pleading with him to change his mind; neither does the Bible suggest Jesus gave an inadequate "altar call." Jesus compared ministry to the planting of good seed in soil of various qualities. The seed is the same but some of the soil is rocky; some of it is shallow; some is thorn-filled; and even good soil brings forth varied harvests of thirty, sixty, or a hundredfold. I must not knock myself over for something I cannot control and for which I have limited responsibility. I grieve for those who do not respond; I pray for them and strongly urge them to follow Christ; but the decision is theirs alone.

I have also learned that although we all have weaknesses we can still bear fruit. God calls only unqualified people—that is all that is available—and he (a) qualifies them in certain ways; and (b) works through them in spite of other incompetencies.

God does not have a single perfect minister. When I moved from the pastorate to editorial work with LEADERSHIP for several years, I interviewed the church leaders whom I had long admired from afar. Up close, I found they are not larger than life. They are good and gifted men and women, worthy of respect, but they too have weaknesses. They too are "jars of clay," whom God uses anyway to display his glory.

And so it has always been. God worked through the apostle Paul even though he apparently was a poor speaker and physically unimpressive. Paul admitted as much to the Corinthians but added that God had given him great knowledge and apostolic authority. God worked through the boldness of Peter, James, and John, though they were uneducated. God worked through the oratory of Spurgeon, though he wrestled regularly with depression. The phrase "God worked in spite of" qualifies every minister who has ever lived.

Not only does God overlook my weaknesses but so do my people. Granted, in every church a few immature people will actually expect a pastor to be perfect, but most do not. I am not fooling anyone in my church; they know my weaknesses quite well, but they have chosen to love and follow me nonetheless. In fact, our weaknesses endear us to people who are only too familiar with their own failings. When good people sense their shepherd loves them and is faithful in service to Christ, they will chuckle over his or her inability to sing, sustain small talk, or organize a banquet. There are limits, of course, and I strive continually for excellence and growth, but most people expect perfection only from those who act as though they're perfect.

Not only can I bear fruit in spite of my inabilities, God uses them for good. I can quickly become independent if I suppose I have it all, but when I am aware of how much I need others, I am forced into greater reliance upon other people and thus a deeper involvement in the community of Christ. My weaknesses also draw out the abilities of others. Churches with an omnicompetent employee for a pastor may have dormant spectators in the pews.

Most importantly, as the apostle Paul describes in his definitive treatise on the subject, I have found my "thorns" keep me humble and cause me to rely more fully on the power of Christ.

For instance, I have more pastoral skills now than when I first entered the ministry, and part of me thinks I know how to pastor a fruitful church. When I came to my present church as the interim, part-time pastor, I served the church only one day a week outside of Sunday. This is not much time to prepare a sermon, keep the church "shop," lead and disciple others. Although I believe in the necessity of prayer, I told the Lord I could not pray as much as I wanted to, that I had to do the minimum of activities to actually pastor the church, and I asked him to make the church fruitful just the same.

Over the first year I think I did a well-qualified job of administration, preaching, and discipleship, but after more than a year I had to face the fact that our meetings lacked the vitality that should characterize a church. With my abilities I could produce neither an ersatz human energy thing nor the real kingdom thing. I finally came face-to-face with what I already knew—for me at least, pastoring abilities cannot substitute for significant prayer—and I rearranged my schedule to let some pastoral tasks slide a bit in order to pray more.

Eight-watt ministry

In 1972 NASA launched the exploratory space probe Pioneer 10. According to Leon Jaroff, in *Time* magazine, the satellite's primary mission was to reach Jupiter, photograph it and its moons, and beam data to earth about the planet's magnetic field, radiation belts, and atmosphere. Scientists regarded this as a bold plan because up until then no satellite had gone beyond Mars, and they feared the asteroid belt would destroy the satellite before it could reach its target.

But Pioneer 10 accomplished its mission and much, much more. Swinging past Jupiter in November 1973, the space probe was hurled at a higher rate of speed toward the edge of the solar system by the planet's immense gravity. At one billion miles from the sun, Pioneer 10 passed Saturn. At some two billion miles, it hurtled past Uranus; Neptune, at nearly three billion miles; Pluto, at almost four billion miles. By 1997, twenty-five years after its launch, Pioneer 10 was more than six billion miles from the sun. And despite that immense distance, Pioneer 10 continues to beam back radio signals to scientists on Earth. "Perhaps most remarkable," writes Jaroff, "is the fact that those signals emanate from an eight-watt transmitter, which radiates about as much power as a bedroom night-light, and take more than nine hours to reach Earth."[1]

"The Little Satellite That Could" was not qualified to do what it did. Engineers designed Pioneer 10 with a useful life of only three years. But it has kept going and going. By simple longevity, its tiny eight-watt transmitter radio accomplished more than anyone thought possible.

So it is when we offer ourselves to serve the Lord. God can work even through someone with eight-watt abilities. God cannot work, however, through someone who quits.

---

[1]Leon, Jaroff, "Still Ticking," *Time* (November 4, 1996): 80.

BROWN-OUT

OF ALL THE DANGERS OF MINISTRY, one I have infrequently dealt with is burnout. I admire those who for whatever reason drive themselves so relentlessly that eventually they turn into a pile of warm ashes—if nothing else, for their dedication and work capacity. As much as I love to work, though, and as much as my romantic soul yearns for the heroic deed, I have never reached the point of near emotional extinction for the cause.

Instead, my downfall has been simply to become worn out to the point where I no longer care, somewhat like a tennis player who after several sets becomes so tired he loses the desire to win. Compared to the tragic drama of burnout, that is decidedly nonheroic.

Someone has said, "Fatigue makes cowards of us all." Let me rephrase that in more general terms: Physical exhaustion alters my emotional state. What I could handle when fresh I no longer feel up to. Difficulties that I first faced like a problem-solver full of faith now cause me to buckle at the knees. The challenges that once energized me now terrify me. While the presenting symptom on such occasions is emotional—depression or weakness—the real problem is physical: low energy.

When I am worn out, the words "I am so tired of . . ." fall easily from my lips. Tired of problems, tired of pressure, tired of sermon deadlines, tired of criticism, tired of working six or seven days a week, tired of difficult people, tired of having everything depend on me, tired of the same place and the same thing, tired of others letting me down. While I feel the problem is what comes at the *end* of the phrase, in reality the word "tired" is the true explanation for my urge to give in.

I have noticed several other characteristics of physical and emotional exhaustion and the desire to quit.

When I want to give up, I often consider more extreme measures than necessary to remedy my situation. When what I may really need is to work only six hours a day for a week to restore my battery, what I imagine I need is a several-week vacation, or a six-month sabbatical, or a new church.

According to the *New York Times*, in March 1997 the forty-nine-year-old CEO of the Luby's Cafeteria chain died of what the police concluded was a suicide. After praying with his wife before going to bed, he slipped out of his house, checked into a motel room, and there slit his own throat. Those who knew him said his actions were completely out of character, and they groped to understand his motives. He had risen through the ranks of the company and only months before had become CEO and president. He was facing his first shareholders meeting a few days hence. Company earnings had declined marginally from when he had taken over, but that was to be expected—so the company's financial picture was anything but disastrous.

Why the bloody suicide then?

As I read the *New York Times* article, I thought to myself that even if he were facing some secret personal disaster, there are better alternatives to suicide. *Anything* is better than that. I wondered if he was worn out, likely doing everything within his power to succeed and prove himself in his new responsibilities. Suicide (or sudden resignation or divorce) is the sort of desperate overreaction carried out by someone who has lost perspective due to emotional and physical exhaustion.

Another effect of wearing out, which I may not recognize as such, is being more easily tempted or provoked. It is as though my body, due to adrenaline or some other chemical stimulus, is in a state of heightened response. A suggestive billboard by the roadside that normally would not get more than a disinterested glance can now awaken a thoughtful look. A critical comment I would usually forbear now angers me. A setback at church or in my finances can quickly lead to despair and doubt. When I am physically and emotionally weak, temptation is strong. For this reason I am especially careful to get a good night's sleep on Saturday. Besides wanting to have maximum energy to preach and minister to people, I have found Sundays always have their share of negatives, whether it be low attendance, a weak sermon, or a fouled-up program. When I am tired, Sundays and Mondays can be devastating. The events of the days themselves do not make them so; my energy level does.

Early in my ministry I read a motivational book in which the author challenged readers with the statement: The world is run by tired people and no one ever died from fatigue. He is right, I thought, and so I drove myself harder and harder to reach my goals, until through hard experience I began to learn some of the repercussions of constant fatigue. Overwork and sleep deprivation may not kill me today, but they can quickly and powerfully harm me emotionally and spiritually. The habitual lack of rest is eventually very destructive, often wiping out the gains from sacrificial hard work.

Why I drive myself

Knowing all these things does not keep me from overwork, however. I still push myself too far on occasion, and when I do, it is usually for one of the following seven reasons:

1. *I work with a humanistic mindset rather than a spiritual one.* Sometimes the way I work for the Lord better resembles the models found in business and motivational literature than the ones in the Bible. At such times, I lose the spirituality of ministry. I do not seek above all to grow in my relationship with God through work; instead, I just want to get work done for its own sake and to reach my goals. I may pray less and depend on technique more, or I pray primarily to get something from God instead of to know him better. My motivation to glorify God and give thanks is weak. I trust in the Lord more to accomplish my dreams than to fulfill his purposes. I "strive in the flesh" rather than rest in God.

When I work with this mindset, overwork is inevitable, for most everything depends on me.

2. *I doubt God will provide for my needs, or I am not content to merely have my needs met.* Because my church cannot afford a full-time pastor, I am bivocational, working the other half of the week as a free-lance writer, which carries no guarantees. Bills, however, are guaranteed—including my health insurance and retirement fund, both of which I pay myself. Consequently, even if I have writing work lined up for several months, I may worry about what happens after that. I feel I cannot let up for even a day because tomorrow I may have no work.

I have the same feeling in pastoral ministry, perhaps because our church averages only thirty-five parishioners. I always think I must work more because we need to grow in strength and next week several people may announce they are moving. Pastoring a church is an entirely unpredictable job, so I need to fish while the water is calm. I lack any sense of security in my church.

3. *I overreach.* What most leads to my depleted reserves are excessive goals, or what some theologians call inordinate desires. The philosophies and clichés carried by the posters of my culture have taken deep root within me. I want to make a difference, be all I can be, dream big dreams, tackle impossible projects. That is good, I guess, but sometimes I want those dreams whether God does or not, and that qualifies as grandiosity. Nothing ups the emotional pressure on me to push, push, push as when I spend time dreaming, goal-setting, and planning.

I love to learn; I can get interested in a multitude of things, and I want to be good at every one of them and become deeply involved in each at the same time. Over the last year, for example, I have flirted with the desires to write my first novel, to write an essay for a secular magazine, to learn to play Bridge, and to get another degree. I have regretted that while I learned to play piano several years ago I have not kept up playing. I have become passionate with a desire to read all the top books on apologetics and one-to-one evangelism; to lead others to a relationship with Christ; to grow in hearing and following the voice of God; to grow in leadership ability and lead our church to great fruitfulness; to enhance my writing skills; to memorize the book of Matthew.

As I hear accounts of churches in America experiencing revival, I want the same for our church, and I want to spend the time in prayer necessary to see this happen.

I want to see my four sons become great servants of Christ, and I want my marriage to glorify the Lord. There are so many good things to do and be in this world, and I want all of it to the maximum.

But big challenges are not all that cause me to overreach. My heart has also felt the twist and churn of envy and self-serving ambition. I am competitive, wanting to do as well or better than every other pastor or writer. When I hear that a church has won many people to Christ, I want to do the same. I don't want to come up short when compared with others.

4. *I become impatient.* Although one of my strengths is patience, some things I long so much to see happen in the short term that I will pay almost any price to hurry them along. One is fruitful evangelism. It seems I want fruitfulness much sooner than God wants it. Presently we are seeing precious few people make the decision to become a Christian, yet I desperately want that to happen more.

Over the last two weeks, for example, what has most challenged my schedule and time constraints has been my desire to bring others to Christ. Two weeks ago we invited to our home a non-Christian couple who were on the top of my list of those with whom I wanted to build a trusting relationship. That of course meant several days of extra work beforehand for my wife and me to get the house and food ready for the occasion. On the Friday we had them over, I left the house at seven in the morning for the church office and did not return until seven that evening. Our guests arrived at eight and stayed until ten-thirty. I felt the effects of this full schedule the next day.

Last Sunday I returned to my office a little after one in the afternoon, following the morning worship service. I ate a bag lunch at my desk and then took care of some administrative duties until three, when I had an appointment I had been anticipating for two weeks. A medical student who had visited our Easter morning service called and asked if I would talk with her boyfriend, who was also a medical student. She told me he was an existentialist, who nevertheless wanted to hear someone explain why Christianity is reasonable.

More than two hours later, when we finished our conversation, I was exhausted but happy beyond words. I had another appointment at six, and our Sunday evening meeting began at six-thirty. I did not regret the tightness of my schedule in the least, however, because I wanted so strongly to tell others about Christ and bring them into a relationship with him. If I could do that every Sunday, I would be ecstatic. I do not want to patiently wait for a few people to come to Christ each year; I want hundreds of people to do so *now*, and I would do almost anything to bring this about.

5. I fall into workaholism. As I write this, I am alone in my house during the dinner hour. This afternoon I said good-bye to my wife and boys as they flew to North Carolina for the wedding of a relative. The trip was provided for my family free of charge, and I could have covered the bases at church to go as well if I had really wanted to go, but I didn't. I do not want to miss a Sunday at my church or a day of writing or a day in the church office. To leave my work behind and go to North Carolina sounded like punishment to me, for I love the work of ministry with an overwhelming love.

Is that workaholism? I have no doubt that sometimes I work too much and attack my to-do list with too much passion. I can find more meaning in my work than in my relationship with God. If I am not accomplishing something, I am miserable.

6. I do not like to take a day off, even a truly restful one. Several years ago I was in a small group with a man who described how taking a true Sabbath had changed his life. "My wife and I used to do many things on Sunday," he said, "but we were tired all week long. Now I am careful to rest deeply on the Sabbath. My wife and I do not shop or run errands or work around the house on Sunday. We have even stopped attending Sunday evening church services. We worship on Sunday morning, and then we rest completely. We have both found that when we do that we have tremendous energy all week; if we do not do this, we drag around all week and simply wait for the week to end.'"

As I considered what he said, I realized my day off was usually an active day. I would have fun at some sporting activity, read, run around doing errands, play with the kids, catch up with whatever was undone, or go out with Nancy. My day off was usually enjoyable but rather tiring, and that fatigue continued through much of the week.

So I forced myself to experiment with doing virtually nothing on my day off, and I discovered why the Jews had trouble keeping the Sabbath. Doing nothing all day is hard, especially in the morning. But I am learning to do so at least once every few weeks. I stay off my feet, spend time in the easy chair, listen to music, hang around with the family. The lure of reading is almost irresistible, but I try to avoid much of that because I do not rest when I read. I concentrate too hard and think of too many other ideas.

I often try to make my day off a Sabbath in the spiritual sense, taking advantage of the disengaged time to listen to God. As the day progresses, I stop thinking of all the things I need to do and eventually take a nap in the early afternoon. As I continue to wind down through the day, I sometimes find I can nap again around dinner. To my surprise, when I go to bed just a bit later than usual, I am able to fall asleep fairly soon and sleep deeply through the night.

When I am able to stick to this regimen (many weeks schedule demands do not allow it, or I feel such restlessness I have to start doing something), I experience a level of physical and emotional renewal that I do not experience otherwise.

7. I press to do things too fast. Earlier in my ministry, I read some literature on time management and got to the place where I tried to squeeze as much as possible into every day. That meant finishing each item on my to-do list as fast as I could. I found, though, that it took all the joy out of my work and, worse yet, it made even short periods of work exhausting because I worked under the self-imposed pressure of deadlines. Instead of enjoying my work, pursuing excellence, and growing in my relationship with God, I merely wanted to get more done. I found that a person can become just as greedy for time and accomplishment as for money. The more you do the more you want to do. Meanwhile I suffered some physical stress symptoms: pain in my jaw and neck, nervousness, and headaches.

After fifteen years, I finally learned that this kind of work pressure is definitely not for me. Now I am more efficient and often work within set parameters for each task. But like my favorite pasta dish, my work is too wonderful a thing to waste on rushing through just to get to the next thing so I can rush through that and get to something else. When I work at the right pace, work is energizing right through to the end of a satisfying day;

when I rush, work quickly becomes stressful and exhausting.

Embrace work with humility

God is teaching me a different model of work and rest than the one found in our secular culture. Work and rest are both spiritual disciplines, dependent upon rhythm and balance, issuing in increasing knowledge of the Father.

Through the spiritual discipline of work, I become an apprentice son who labors side by side with his diligent, always productive Father. I discover the unique joy only a working relationship can bring, for no relationship matches the satisfaction known by two who work together well. In the process, the Father trains my soul in right motivations and steely character as each new challenge demands more dependence upon him, the source of wisdom and diligence, faithfulness and persistence. Being involved in spiritual work, I must breathe the Spirit, think and pray in the Spirit. Indeed, spirituality becomes my requisite "skill." For co-workers with the Father the secular idea of empowerment takes on a whole new meaning.

On the other hand, the spiritual discipline of rest offers a different sort of empowerment. It brings physical and emotional restoration, which is necessary, but more important to me spiritually is the fact that I receive through rest a regular reminder of my place in God's economy, and there I can find contentment. "Be still, and know that I am God" (Ps. 46:10). The discipline of rest shows that God has set boundaries on my life: the limitations of time and energy. To acknowledge without resentment the weakness of my humanity is to honor God as divine. God is unlimited in nature; I am not. He does great things; I do not. He is the Messiah; I am not. These truths wash anew upon the shore of my heart when I rest. While work teaches me what I *can* do, rest teaches me what I *cannot* do. If I have prayed and fulfilled my responsibilities, I will see what the mighty One can do without me.

Consequently the discipline of Sabbath (on whatever day and for whatever length of time), which means complete rest for the Lord's sake, glorifies God. Through rest I show my trust in the One who can accomplish more in a moment than I can in a thousand lifetimes. Through rest I prove my belief in Him whose blessing truly makes rich. Instead of unstinting toil done out of the fear that I will one day suffer want, through rest I express my dependence upon the God of Abraham, Yahweh Jireh. Instead of ministering eighty hours a week as though everything depended upon me, through rest I convey that the kingdom depends upon God. My hands folded in Sabbath rest praise the One who opens his hands and satisfies the desire of every living thing.

If I cannot rest, I betray an inflated view of my own importance. The discipline of rest is a regular embrace with humility, through which my soul, often striving and straining like a dog on a leash, finds peace.

After taking Mondays off for quite a period of time, I recently moved my Sabbath to Saturday, and the difference this has made in my week has surprised me. When

I took Mondays off, I basically spent much of the day in emotional and physical torpor, recovering from the intense preparation for Sunday and the experience of it. (Because I serve our church only part time, I spend my entire Sunday in morning and evening services, afternoon leadership meetings, and office work.) Far from finding any pleasure in Mondays, depressing as they were, I actually dreaded my day off.

Taking Mondays off had another drawback: Sunday followed five days of work, meaning I operated on depleted energy reserves and often felt frazzled. I sometimes found myself fumbling for syntax and words and inspiration in my sermons—a sure sign of mental exhaustion. With Saturdays off, I find the rhythm of my schedule, my emotions, and my physical energy far more favorable. On Sundays I am brimming with a sense of well-being; in the pulpit I am fresh and spontaneous; I have my legs throughout the service and to the end of the day. On Mondays I awake with anticipation to tie up loose ends from Sunday and plan the week ahead. And, wonder of wonders, Saturdays have become enjoyable, positive days off with my family.

I have found the wise balance of rest and work determines my effectiveness almost as much as the diligence with which I pray. Work and rest are indeed spiritual disciplines.

AFTER THE REVOLT

AS A PASTOR, ASIDE FROM occasional criticism, I have faced only one full-blown revolt. Trouble was afoot but everything *seemed* quite normal—for a while. Then increasingly disconcerting things began to happen. I kept saying to myself, *No, that noise in the basement can't be an intruder.* Eventually I learned otherwise. When the truth started coming out, it read like the first chapter of a horror story.

In conversations with leaders, I began to hear reports of criticism against me. One individual spoke face-to-face with me on several occasions about shortcomings he saw in the church, adding that he had also discussed these problems with others. In one worship service as we waited quietly before the Lord, this man began to pray so loudly it was unsettling, and judging by the looks on the faces of the congregation, I wasn't the only one who thought so. I didn't want to confront him openly, so I quickly ended the worship portion of the service and moved on. Then a man who was a former pastor stood and corrected the younger man for being out of order. I expressed my agreement. We continued the service but limped our way through to the end.

Then things worsened. A few people who were involved in ministry stopped attending our church. Criticism even surfaced against my family. Piecing together who hung around with whom, I figured the revolt involved about ten dissidents, with at least four leaders among them. I realized then that this would not simply go away.

The nadir of the revolt was a meeting I had with two leaders. They phoned my office one day and asked if they could come right over and talk. When they arrived, I greeted them warmly, but they were not smiling. They handed me several sheets of paper listing my failings as a pastor. Seated across from me, they worked their way through the list, explaining each of my faults. As I recall, I did not verbally respond to the specifics. When they were done, I thanked them and said I would pray about their observations. Then I told them their ministry in the church would be put on hold until the issues were resolved.

At that point one of the individuals exploded in anger. By the time he finished with what he had to say, he was leaning across my desk and screaming in my face.

Special effects

Conflict throws a wrench into the challenge of perseverance. My emotional response to this revolt was threefold.

1. *Fatigue and discouragement.* In high school gym class, the activity I enjoyed least was wrestling. I will never forget the feeling I had when we progressed beyond takedowns and holds and held a class tournament. Despite the shortness of the matches and the fact that I trained year-round in gymnastics, I quickly became exhausted. Midway through the match, whether on top or underneath, I wanted the match to end.

Similarly, I found church conflict to be exhausting. Confrontations affected me at a visceral level. At the speed of a nerve impulse, they triggered insecurity; they challenged my worth and ability; they ignited response mechanisms of self-defense. The aftereffect of these high-adrenaline events was low-level energy.

Needless to say, the exhaustion hampered my work. Occasionally, I found myself staring at the office walls or at papers on my desk without the creativity to write a sermon or the willpower to make a decision. I wept easily; I felt depressed; I was preoccupied.

2. *Emotional shutdown.* During the conflict, the strength of my feelings scared me. I had come to one firm resolve: no matter what happened to me, the one thing I would not do in this crisis was sin against God. My emotions threatened to undo my resolve.

Like a flood victim caught in a rushing torrent, on occasion I felt carried away by circumstances beyond my control. I had to defend against the pain, so when things became intense I went Spock, disengaging emotionally. Even when I could not control my circumstances, I *could* control my emotions, so I shut down and tried not to care too much. Stoically I did my best to engage life on the level of reason; in analysis I found solace and escape.

3. Conflict-generated energy. I become bored if I play chess with someone who does not understand the principles of the game. Though I would be a pushover for a dedicated player, I have read several chess books and know the fundamental tenets, such as the need to develop all pieces early, control the center of the board, keep a strong pawn skeleton, and maximize the mobility of your pieces. It is impossible for a novice to beat a player who understands these ideas. As a result, I lose interest in a game with a learner. But when I get the opportunity to play a quality player, every cell in my brain awakens. Competition always brings out the best in me, as well as an almost intoxicating joy.

In a church conflict, the stakes are immeasurably higher. In this crisis I planned to fight it out to the end—not against people but for God's purpose. The greater the challenge the better. I especially felt this way around others because I wanted to be a strong leader. I even alienated my wife a few times when she felt discouraged and needed to talk about the situation: I brushed her off with glib comments that downplayed the crisis; I wanted to talk positively about it. My pulpit presence was usually confident, more so than before the trouble broke out. In public meetings I went out of my way to show others I was not about to be beaten. I *would lead the church* through this crisis. I would be a rock when everything else gave way.

I did make some adjustments, though. Since my

vision had provoked some of the conflict, I gradually backed off. As I saw it, we would have to hold the fort for six months to a year and then we would rebuild. I knew that every church faces periods of testing and that most pastors who take over an existing church have to weather some conflict in the first five years. War has casualties but we would pass this test. I was prepared to pay the price and stay for the long haul.

Distorted perseverance

Consequently I was able to stay at the church and function effectively most of the time. I do not recall ever seriously considering a search for another church. The test was not my ability to stay at the church but rather the purity of my motivations. Conflict lured me at times into a distorted perseverance in which I sometimes hung tough for the wrong reasons.

I occasionally persevered for the sake of persevering. Right or wrong, I could be content with mere survival, wearing my survivor's badge with pride. The benefit of this thinking was resilience, but it was easy to take my eyes off the broader strategic questions: How can we move toward effective ministry for Christ? What are the Lord's ultimate purposes for us? What can we do to fulfill those purposes?

Another distorted motivation for perseverance was the subtle desire to prove myself right. To do so I determined to outlast my detractors and see the blessing of God upon the church. I recall a bit of cold calculation on my part: I was here before they were. I have the pulpit, the keys, the position. I have more control than anyone. They lack vested interest in this church. Eventually they will lose interest and go elsewhere.

In other words, I wanted to be the one holding the reins in the end. Though fallible, I felt I had authority from God as the pastor to see that his will prevailed, and I sincerely felt I was following God's purposes. Even so, it was hard to separate between my being right and God's being right. But I was fully aware of this.

The conflict also caused me to waver on some essential responsibilities. The first was my obligation to shepherd my detractors. Instead of a desire to help them grow through the experience, at times I abandoned them—at least in my heart. They had hurt me badly enough and troubled the church sufficiently that I simply wanted them to be gone.

In retrospect, I realize I shouldn't be surprised when sheep act like sheep. In the days before his crucifixion, with full knowledge that a disciple would betray him and the others would leave him to fend for himself, Jesus continued to instruct and prepare them for the future. I am supposed to act like the Good Shepherd, not a bad sheep. In theory, I should have more spiritual resources than my detractors do to weather a conflict and come out the stronger. Spiritually, they may never recover. Even if they do not respond to my leadership and will probably leave the church, I need to be trustworthy. I need to sow as many seeds of wisdom into their hearts for the future as possible. I must hope they will later see their mistakes and never repeat them in another church. I need to persevere as a shepherd.

While at Arlington Heights, I succeeded at this with only one person who had actively opposed me. He was extremely dedicated to the Lord but had a huge blind spot: he saw nothing wrong with stirring church dissent. After church services he would talk with friends about the church's failings and admitted as much to me.

I liked him, nevertheless, and saw his potential. So I met with him many times in my office for a full hearing on what concerned him. I admitted my fallibility to him but said I felt I was walking in God's steps. Not just for my own sake but for his, I confronted him about his negative talk with others. I showed him Scripture passages on the errors of divisiveness.

He listened quietly but never changed his actions. Finally I realized that for both the church's sake and for his, and in accordance with Titus 3:10, I had to be ready to place him under church discipline. In another meeting in my office, I warned that if he continued to stir up trouble he would be disciplined. Regrettably, he continued, and I had to tell him he was no longer welcome in our church. He stopped attending, and I have no idea what happened to him after that.

When guns fall silent

I had it easy; the revolt lasted only five months and virtually all the dissidents left the church. We did suffer a major reversal, however, as the church dropped in attendance by 40 percent and we lost most of our core workers. Undaunted, I pressed on for six months after the smoke cleared, but as time passed I could not help but notice some enduring troubles. Church attendance plateaued and, far worse, the congregation seemed to have lost heart.

Recently I read an article about what makes a soldier willing to face combat. It said that a military unit that suffers two or more battles incurring a large ratio of casualties will become demoralized. Our church had suffered major casualties *before* I came as pastor, and it seemed now to have reached its limit. Our meetings felt hollow and we had only an occasional visitor. My wife and I both felt like a lid was on the congregation—God was not getting through, and consequently not blessing our efforts.

I began to wonder if I had missed God's direction the year before. At that time LEADERSHIP had asked me to consider coming to work as an associate editor for the magazine, and I had declined. God apparently wanted to give me a second chance. One year after the conflict began, the editor called again to ask me to reconsider. This time I felt all signs pointed to a change.

Problems of any sort raise key questions about perseverance. How can I know whether the troubles I currently suffer are a circumstantial sign from God that he has a new direction for me? How do I know if my circumstances are something God wants me to endure and then grow through?

Only through prayer can we find the answers to these questions. As strongly as I believe in perseverance, I do believe there are times when we need to move on, especially in a conflictual situation. If LEADERSHIP had not called me and the climate at the church had lingered, I would have eventually pursued another place of ministry. I had learned a lesson from a pastor friend who had faced recurrent opposition. He had pastored his church following an immensely popular founding pastor, and for more than ten years he saw several waves of revolt and departure. A man of impeccable character, he was determined to work through it, but eventually church attendance dropped by three-fourths and he had to leave. Sometimes conflict can so muddy the waters that a pastor's ministry can never recover in the place where the conflict occurred.

In my idealism I want to see conflict and criticism as an anomaly in the life of the body, something like appendicitis. But in Scripture I see a different picture. In the lives of Jesus and Paul, opposition came with the frequency of a cold. Realistically I must have the ability to keep doing God's will in a conflict, and so hopefully prevail in further productive ministry.

In fact, judging by the Beatitudes, perseverance in conflict is not only a key to pastoral fruitfulness but also to spirituality. The Beatitudes major in issues related to conflict. Three of the eight beatitudes speak directly to it: "Blessed are the meek. Blessed are the peacemakers. Blessed are those who are persecuted because of righteousness." Four more have strong relevance: "Blessed are the merciful. Blessed are the pure in heart. Blessed are those who mourn. Blessed are those who hunger and thirst for righteousness." Apparently, though a conflict situation feels like a spiritual vacuum as cold and dark as deep space, it is actually a spiritual hothouse for a more vigorous brand of spirituality.

In many ways the conflicts that call for my perseverance are defining moments in my ministry. They are passages that either lead me to a higher plane in Christ or shove me headlong down the stairs. They promote either godliness or bitterness; they reveal to me more of God or more of my sinful self. In my experience they have done a measure of both, but over time the positive has significantly outweighed the negative. With God's help, I can overcome evil with good.

6

EXPECTATION MANAGEMENT

ONE HEARTRENDING TELEVISION PROFILE during the 1996 Atlanta Summer Olympics told of a United States wrestler who for years had dominated meet after meet and now was expected to win a gold medal. Sadly, though, with family, friends, team, and country rooting for him, he lost one of the early rounds.

At the completion of his match, this tough wrestler was so distraught he fell to his knees with his face to the mat and wept like a baby. His teammates tried to lift him from the mat, but he refused to rise. Finally he got up and trudged off, head down, grieving as if he had lost a loved one.

Expectations are powerful. They touch deep emotional currents. They affect our personal dreams and values, our relationships. They can define our work and responsibilities. In short, they can control us.

Usually the power of expectation is beneficial; other times it can put us into a painful realm where no one can live happily. This is the place of unrealistic expectations—the ones we put on ourselves as well as the ones others place on us. Perhaps no group is more susceptible to this position than pastors, and no matter how spiritual we are, it can kill our desire to go on.

I know. I've been there. I do not recall, now, the specific criticism leveled against me, but I felt that at the root of it was an unfair expectation and I was smarting from it. As I drove home, I defended myself: *How can I do more than I am already doing? I work sixty hours a week. I fast and pray one day a week. I study hard for each sermon. I don't even have a secretary.* When I got home I continued to mull over what had been said to me.

This was not a propitious time for my wife to point out a task I had failed to do at home, but she did. I exploded. I catalogued the demands I was trying to meet and the people I was trying to please—including her and our boys. I moaned about how impossible my responsibilities were, then marched off to another room. *Phooey on everyone!* I thought. *If they don't like me the way I am, tough.*

After I got over the temporary insanity of anger, I apologized to Nancy and put the comments from those at church in perspective. I wish I could say that such an episode has happened only once, but that is not the case. In my first two pastorates, it happened every year or two. The intensity of my explosion varied, but the common ingredient was unrealistic expectations.

And there have been many. At times I have expected myself to excel at every facet of ministry. To read whatever people hand to me. To make my church as fruitful as other churches. To be available at every moment. To be both here and there at the same time. To offer programs for every group in the congregation. To have a perfect church.

One classic video game that gives me fits is Missile Command. On the bottom of the screen, there are six cities and three defensive missile launching sites. From the top of the screen, waves of missiles rain down to destroy them. The object of the game is defense and survival: destroy the falling explosives before they destroy you.

I quickly learned to handle the first level without any challenge. The bombs fall slowly and are few in number. I destroy them with ease, the bombardment ends, and my score is tallied. I can handle this.

Then a jarring alarm sounds. With the second level the difficulty escalates noticeably. More bombs fall—faster. I can beat this level with a sense of control, but by the end I know I have been tested.

With the increasing difficulty of the third and fourth levels, I begin to lose control. There are more bombs. These split halfway down into still more bombs and they plummet at even faster speeds. Soon I cannot deliberately aim and shoot but only fire wildly in the hope of hitting something. One or two bombs get through, taking out a city or missile site and cutting down my defense capabilities.

The annoying alarm sounds at each new level. Then I face the added difficulty of smart bombs, which dodge my missiles—unless I make a direct hit. Soon my strategy is to defend only a few cities and an adjacent missile site. Finally the onslaught is physically impossible to withstand. My cities and missile sites have become craters. The game is over.

Somehow the game reminds me of my life as a pastor.

First, my expectations escalate. If I meet one goal, I set a higher one. I want to preach better; I want to pray more. The more I plan, the more my work multiplies. When I meet the expectations of others, my responsiveness encourages some people to demand even more. Beating level two only brings on level three.

Second, the more I press to meet unrealistic expectations, the less control I feel. During one year, the expectations were so numerous I merely made desperate, heroic efforts in a lost battle. I threw some time and energy at one problem, hoping my sacrifice would remedy the situation; then I swung my attention in another direction, throwing myself at another demand.

Third, the alarm keeps sounding. In Missile Command I concentrate so hard on the screen I am not conscious of the jarring tones. But they amplify the emotional state of the crisis. In ministry when I determine that, live or die, I am going to reach my goals, solve all the problems, or keep everyone happy, my stress multiplies exponentially.

Unrealistic expectations curtail the joy and often the longevity of ministry. They can cause me to give up either in deed or in heart. I don't have to resign to quit. I can simply decide this job is impossible and it is foolish to try.

In a conversation with a leader about the pastoral role I had, he at one point asked, "Has the church created a job that no one can do?"

I don't think so. If I have *realistic* expectations, pastoral ministry is something I can do—do well and do happily (I now enjoy ministry beyond words). The culprit is *unrealistic* expectations.

Here is the irony: For years, whenever I suffered a stressed-out episode, I assumed others were forcing impossible demands on me. But I finally realized that *I* was the one putting on the pressure: I assumed it was my job to keep so-and-so happy; I had to read so many books a year; I had to invest a minimum of so many hours in every sermon; I had to reach goals set arbitrarily months before. The impossible situations were of my own making.

When I simply could not keep going, however, and occasionally gave up on an expectation—behold, the world did not end. Ministry continued—often better than before. My state of alarm was a self-induced emergency I could turn off as easily as a computer game. Perhaps the easiest thing to do in pastoral ministry is to give up our unrealistic expectations!

So why have I not always done so?

Caving in

The last term I would use to describe my preaching is *prophetic*. I assume most Christians need understanding and encouragement more often than a kick in the pants. I recall preaching one sermon, though—in my first church—in which I really let the congregation have it. Afterward a woman thirty years my senior approached me with an enthusiastic smile on her face. "Great sermon!" she said. "I love that kind of preaching."

I wish she had not told me that. For the next several weeks I tried to preach more scorching messages. *This is what's been missing,* I thought. Preaching that way felt macho and, consciously or not, I wanted to please this woman and others like her. If I preached in a manner hearers "enjoyed," I figured the church would grow. As it turned out, my first scorcher may have been a necessary wake-up call, but the ones that followed did not wear well, and I soon reverted to my natural style.

Red-faced, I must admit this story typifies my first few years as a pastor. To a large extent, I wanted to please people and to be liked. I yearned for church growth and thought keeping people happy was the secret. With a philosophy of ministry based largely on the principle of attraction, I was an easy mark for the unrealistic expectations of others.

I don't think I wanted to please people more than the Lord, but I thought pleasing them was a way to please him. Unselfishness meant, more often than not, yielding to others. Having good feelings in church felt more Christian to me than saying no to people.

Someone has said Christians fall into two groups: the love camp and the truth camp. The latter value right and wrong, living the truth and telling the truth. The love camp, on the other hand, majors in feelings between people. It seems logical to me that this group is more likely to bend to unrealistic expectations. Granted, this is an oversimplification, but I think there is some truth to it. Apparently I have leaned toward the love camp. I didn't know there was any other way to function. It was who I was.

But I am learning. My hiatus from the pastorate as an editor made me aware of this tendency and its downfalls. I saw other leadership styles and the benefits of balancing my desire for good feelings between people with the need for truth-telling and occasional confrontation. Also, living for a few years without the expectations of a church, I realized how beholden I had become to the expectations of others. For the first time in over a decade I felt free to be myself. I began to care less about what others thought of me and more about what I felt was right. If others did not like me, that was the price I had to pay for being true to what I felt God wanted me to do or be.

In addition, God has been speaking to me about this issue. Over the last two years, as I have waited upon God, listening for his voice in Scripture and in prayer, the word most frequently impressed upon my heart has been "truth." I am putting this new emphasis into action in the church. Several times in my present pastorate I have made it a point to confront people when necessary.

I have also come to the realization that trying to build a church largely by pleasing people and seeking to attract them to the church—catering to the consumer mentality—is in the long-run spiritually destructive. While this is true for many transcendent reasons, pragmatically it is so because if we try to please someone who is not aligned with the firm vision and values of our fellowship, we only set ourselves up for conflict later. If new people are not drawn by what we truly are and believe, it is better if they do not remain with us.

Another culprit in my tendency to bend to unrealistic expectations has been the nature of my relationship with God. I know my salvation is based on grace alone, but my daily relationship with the Lord has often been focused on performance. I have been compelled to work *for* him. Is this zeal, bad theology, or a distortion in my personality?

Probably all of the above. I know I am saved by grace, but various truths sometimes overshadow that, and I unconsciously feel as though God will not smile on how I live by grace. For example, the New Testament abounds with references to both grace and responsibility—actions that please and actions that displease God. I am a steward of much and accountable for it all. If I love as Christ loved, I don't merely say nice words, I give my life to others. I will be judged and rewarded for my works. Faith without works is dead. What this all means is that I sometimes confuse the basis of my relationship with God—his love and grace and the work of Christ—with the responsibility I have for how I live. But they are two different things.

My orientation toward performance in my relationship with God finds expression in numerous ways. In prayer, I may spend more time in confession of sinful attitudes and petition for what I want to see accomplished than I do in the enjoyment of intimacy with God. Regarding the values that drive me, I have always worked to lay up treasures in heaven. In ministry, when the church goes poorly, I can feel that God is unhappy with what I am doing, and when the church goes well, I feel he is pleased with me. In short, I can live as though the harder I work, the more blessed I will be.

The problem also stems from my personality. No matter what some say about unconditional love and acceptance from God or others, in the depths of my soul I don't always buy it. Besides the fact that performance makes me feel good about myself, I also think performance makes others feel good about me. It seems that people most respect, value, and love those who perform well.

There have been periods in my life when I have fallen prey to the Rudolph-the-Red-Nosed-Reindeer syndrome. In the reindeer pecking order, Rudolph was a nobody. Then came that foggy Christmas Eve, when Rudolph had an ability that others valued—a nose that glowed in the dark. After he saved Christmas, the song says, "Then all the reindeer loved him. . . ."

I thought that if "my nose glowed in the dark," I would be accepted and loved. This mentality seems to be driven by the real world. The world revolves around performance: do what others value to earn money and pay the bills; express love to family and friends to have healthy relationships. On occasion, that assumption has even affected my relationship with God. With so much at stake in how I viewed performance at these times of imbalance, I easily became a slave to unrealistic expectations of myself on a spiritual level.

When I brought things back into perspective, I realized that performance is important, but it is only part of what defines me and only a portion of what brings me into loving relationships with others.

A final reason why I have been swayed by high expectations in the past has been a sense of insecurity as a pastor: I have feared losing people from our church. I have felt that if I bungle ministry to individuals in even minor ways, they will go elsewhere. I have frequently resembled the self-employed person who never says no to work—no matter how much is on his plate—for fear that in three weeks he will not have work to do.

In my first pastorate, for example, I did not have a secretary, nor did I have a answering machine. If I left the office, the phone was not answered. As time went on this thought bothered me more and more. While on hospital calls, church errands, or home visitation, I would think about members calling the office and, not getting an answer, assuming I was at home with my feet up, sipping coffee.

For several months this concern was exacerbated by one woman who, it seemed to me, had concluded I was not working hard enough. I would receive several pointless phone calls from her at the office in the morning and then again late in the afternoon. Occasionally she would mention that she had tried to reach me at another time and no one had answered. Sometimes, with her in mind, I would be almost driven to hurry to the office in the morning so as not to miss her call and be found truant. But even though she brought me such anxiety, I did not want her to leave the church. To me, the worst thing that could happen would be for someone to leave the church.

I have a greater sense of security now. And though our church is small in number and therefore keenly feels the negative effect of a lost attendee, if people move on I can trust God to replace them. This is God's church, not my church. My reputation and my financial needs are also God's responsibility. Jesus said he would build his church. So even if our church were to suffer a temporary downswing, I refuse to worry about it. My life and our church are in God's hands.

Distinctions that bring joy

Dealing with exaggerated expectations, I have learned to make a few key distinctions:

There is a difference between slavishly pleasing people and doing what is worthy of respect. The latter is valid and necessary. For instance, my office day begins at 8:15 in the morning.

There is a difference between realistic and unrealistic expectations. I must take seriously the legitimate demands of my role and not merely please myself. Recently, because of my part-time status, a man in our church asked me to publish in the bulletin each week what my hours would be for that week. I decided this was a legitimate request and began doing it.

There is a difference between the expectations others put on me and the ones I imagine they have put on me. For example, I preached every Sunday in 1996 (because I serve the church half-time, I do not have any vacation days). No one said I had to preach every Sunday, but I don't want anyone to get the feeling they are not getting their "money's worth."

Several months ago I was writing at home shortly

after lunch, when one of the men from church called. "I hate to do this," he said, "but I need to ask if you can do me a favor. If you say no, I will understand and will find another way."

"Go ahead," I said.

"I had surgery yesterday on my sinuses," he said, "and I am having some problems. It's not an emergency, but I need to go to the hospital where I had the surgery and have them take a look at me. But I can't drive. I'm wondering if you can take me. If you can't, I'll take a taxi."

"Let me think a moment," I replied.

Although the hospital was an hour's drive away, I wanted to help Joe if I could. Besides my desire to help someone I care about, I had been preaching about building community for months, and this would be a great opportunity to teach by example. However, this situation was an interruption to my work. What I was doing was urgent, and if I were to drive Joe to the hospital, my wife would have to leave work early to be with the children.

As I weighed my decision, I consciously told myself something I don't think I've ever said before: *I am free to go either way with this. If helping Joe will put too much hardship on me and my family, I am willing to turn him down and face the repercussions in the unlikely event he is offended (I knew him to be a mature person). If I choose to help, I will do so because I want to, not because I have to.*

I decided I wanted to do it. My wife was able to cover the bases at home, and I left to get Joe by midafternoon. I returned home around ten at night but I did not feel upset about it. I was glad to be able to help a brother in need.

Managing unrealistic expectations does not necessarily mean doing less. It means doing the extras willingly—with freedom and joy rather than because I must do them. When I minister like this, I feel I can pastor this church for the rest of my life.

7

MINDING MY OWN BUSINESS

ONE SUMMER HOLIDAY, when I was around nine years old, another family visited our home. As we barbecued burgers in the backyard that afternoon, the father of the other family began to wrestle with his sons in the grass. The boys climbed on his back and held on to his legs as he fought them off like an embattled bear. Then he picked them up and spun them around like airplanes. My father was busy with something at the time, and as I watched the other family I felt left out. *My father doesn't wrestle with me like that*, I thought. And in a rush of deep sadness I childishly concluded that those boys had a better father than I did. I went sulking to my room, and then later tearfully told my mother and father how I felt.

The truth was, my father and I did many great things together. He took me to White Sox, Bears, and Bulls games. We played baseball together, and he attended many of my Little League games. He never spoke a critical word to me, but rather affirmed me often. He provided a comfortable suburban life for our family of eight.

Nevertheless, at that moment of narrow comparison, I overlooked all his virtues and the good things he did for me and focused on the one thing I wanted at the time. I drank the poison of envy.

Comparisons are deceptively skewed, and in this case, tragically so. Perhaps a year or so after the holiday we shared with this family, the father I had so admired committed suicide. My father and I continue to be the greatest of friends to this day.

Not all comparisons are foolish but they can be destructive. They have plagued me in my position as a pastor no less than they do the ambitious corporate executive who compares his office with a co-worker's down the hall. In fact, in my judgment, one of the most besetting sins in my life has been my tendency to irrationally compare myself with others.

No doubt the most raging struggles came during my first pastorate in Chicago, when I was young, out to prove myself, and apparently falling short of my peers. A medical chart would have shown a monthly spike in my blood pressure on the day of the denominational fellowship meeting, when I frequently compared myself with the other pastors. Typically, I began feeling depressed during my drive to the suburban meeting as I became aware of the immaculate surroundings and compared them to my church location. Over coffee, when my peers reported good success in their churches, I felt like a failure. When they talked about vacations, I thought about how I could not afford to take one. When they expressed gratitude for strong leaders or contributors in their churches, I felt sorry for myself as a pastor in a poor Chicago neighborhood. When another rookie pastor was asked to read Scripture, I wondered why I was not selected. In my mind, I was always on the short end of things.

This state of mind lingered as I drove home from these fellowship meetings. I would suffer abysmal despair and depression and languish for the rest of the day and often into the next, wishing I could either succeed or move. Only when I turned my thoughts away from my peers and focused them on what God had given me to do would my faith and determination recover.

In short, I have the dubious honor of being an expert on relentless comparison. Here are seven things I have learned.

1. *Comparisons make even the most advantaged persons feel dissatisfied.* Comparisons lead to dissatisfaction because they are relative; no matter how well off we are, someone else always has more. Professional athletes have taken this to obscene limits. The average guy can only shake his head at the professional athlete with a $20 million contract who threatens to go elsewhere next season because a player on another team makes $22 million. "It's not about money," the grim-faced athlete says to the news camera, "it's about respect."

What scares me is that I have the same sinful nature as these guys do. In their sneakers, I would have the same inclinations. As a pastor I do similar things on a smaller scale. Just as a greedy person can never have enough money, a pastor who compares himself to other pastors can never have enough of whatever it is he longs for.

2. *Inappropriate comparisons focus on what we don't have rather than on what we have.* Ahab, king of Samaria, had a lot: money, power, land, and more. One day, though, he realized that the vineyard of his neighbor, Naboth, would make a nice royal garden. He set his heart on it and made an offer: "Let me have your vineyard to use for a vegetable garden," said Ahab, "since it is close to my palace. In exchange I will give you a better vineyard or, if you prefer, I will pay you whatever it is worth."

That sounds fair, doesn't it? Perhaps, to we moderns, but we have little or no grasp of the significance of an inheritance to an Israelite. To Naboth, this was not merely property; this was his family's inheritance from Yahweh, going back generations. This land represented their security, their heritage. A noble Israelite did not off-handedly sell a few acres of his inheritance and buy something else.

Thus with shuddering revulsion, Naboth replied, "The Lord forbid that I should give you the inheritance of my fathers."

Ahab went home sullen and angry, like a spoiled rich child whose mother had refused him a candy bar in the checkout line. Ahab lay on his bed feeling sorry for himself. He was oblivious to his vast holdings and was fixated on a little patch of potential garden.

Such is the pathetic sight of an advantaged person who has indulged in irrational comparison. I see myself in that picture and it disgusts me. God has blessed me beyond description, yet somehow I find a way to want what others have. When will I be content? When will I be grateful enough for what God has given me that I can rejoice without envy in the blessings he gives to others? "What a wretched man I am! Who will rescue me from this body of death?"

3. Inappropriate comparison is selective and therefore deceptive. I fool myself when I compare myself with a few desirable aspects of someone else's life, blissfully ignorant of the undesirable side. Do I *really* want to step into that person's shoes?

In the initial years of my ministry, I occasionally indulged in the folly of selective comparison with none other than our district superintendent. When I watched him lead district denominational meetings, I sometimes thought it would be great to have his position. He was a respected leader with wide influence; I was a youthful nobody with small influence. His would be the life.

Over the years, however, I have heard enough stories to know what a painful responsibility a district superintendent has. Granted, he yields great influence, and a few times a year he can preach to a thousand or so leaders, but normally he deals with conflict, with the dark side of church leaders. Compare that with the joyful opportunities I have to help lead unbelievers to Christ, to disciple Christians, to open weekly the Word of God and give spiritual food to the same community of faith. I go to a district meeting today and feel sorry for anyone who must leave the joys of frontline pastoral ministry for the position of district superintendent.

4. Inappropriate comparisons divert me from what God wants me to do. One question I long to ask the Lord is whether I missed his best when I left my pastorate in inner-city Chicago for suburban Arlington Heights. I pastored in Chicago eight years, much of the time feeling trapped, even though I loved the people and the church made progress. Raised in the suburbs, I never fully adjusted to inner-city life. Consequently I complained often to the Lord and envied suburban pastors. I assumed they had it good: money, nice buildings, more receptive people (I thought). With my attitude, it is not surprising that when the district superintendent called one day with the opportunity for me to pastor in the suburbs, though the church was a struggling work of thirty-five, I made the move.

At the time, I felt many factors pointed to this as the will of God, but now I wonder. The first three years in Arlington Heights were in my view virtually wasted. People came and went, but I cannot point to many changed lives. In addition, the church I left in Chicago suffered terrible upheaval with my successor, from which it took years to recover. On the surface at least, the move did more harm than good.

Below the surface things did not fare much better. The longer I pastored in Arlington Heights, the more I longed to return to Chicago, where my heart beat with true spiritual passion. From the start I knew I lacked a deep spiritual concern for the people in Arlington Heights, the kind of concern that comes only from God. That is especially evident to me now, as I am back pastoring in Chicago, where I feel a perfect fit in my spirit, a contentment that no matter what happens I am where God wants me to be. And that is what matters. Perhaps God let me go to Arlington Heights to teach me some lessons, but I am fairly certain my relentless comparing had something to do with the move.

5. Not all comparisons are bad. While comparisons harm us in many ways, certainly some are helpful. Pinned to my basement wall is a life-size poster of All-Star Chicago Bear linebacker Mike Singletary. Printed along the length of one side are rule marks so my son could measure his growth compared to his hero. When he stood as straight and tall as he could beside the poster, he enjoyed an inspirational comparison. Comparisons benefit us when we look up to others as good examples, models, or leaders.

Many people do that for me. I listen to PREACHING TODAY sermons monthly, and sometimes when a tape ends I immediately insert one of my own sermons to compare. I have found that if I only critique myself against myself, I can grow accustomed to serious—yet correctable—weaknesses. For example, several months ago another preacher's message caused me to realize my sense of urgency had diminished. As a result, I intentionally worked on better preparation of my heart before preaching. Though I have outgrown the urge to imitate outstanding preachers, many teach and challenge me by the quality of their ministry.

One difference between beneficial and inappropriate comparison, then, is my attitude toward the other person. Do I respect and admire him, or do I have a sense of competition and envy toward him?

6. To overcome irrational comparisons I must call them what they are. Though not entirely free of envy, I rarely suffer from the feverish form of comparing that I did early in my ministry, and this is largely due to one experience. One day I came home from a minister's meeting quite depressed, and as I thought about my feelings, for the first time I saw them for what they were. *This is envy*, I realized. It is hard to imagine this had never occurred to me before, but I had been blinded by self-pity. I had not previously seen my comparing as sinful. When I feel sorry for myself, envy somehow seems justified.

As I called these feelings what they were, however, I crossed a great divide. For the first time, I saw what I was doing in the light of Scripture. In Paul's list of the acts of the sinful nature in Galatians 5:19–21, for example, I saw envy and selfish ambition mentioned in the same breath as orgies, idolatry, and witchcraft! I realized I had a serious problem—sin—that simply had to stop. Selfish comparison with others always leads to sin. If I come up short, I fall to envy; if I come up tall, I sink into arrogance.

"Sin" was not the only word that gave me pause. I also came to the point of calling my bad habit by a word that had an even stronger impact on me: "evil." I now clearly saw my constant comparing as an expression of doubt: questioning God's sovereignty and goodness and wisdom. It was a form of spiritual adultery: lusting for advantages God had not granted me. An expression of coveting what God had granted others. I saw the practice as gangrenous; I was hindering the well-being of others and it made me sad. I saw it as ambitious, for I yearned to succeed for my own sake and surpass my brothers.

I saw the whole wretched thing as a disease of the spirit that does great harm to others in the church of

Jesus Christ. When the fever hit Corinth, it tore the church apart. When Cain compared himself with Abel, he came up short, wanted more, and committed murder. When Saul compared himself with David, he eventually became subject to evil spirits and tried to murder David. When Satan compared himself with God, he didn't measure up, wanted to be exalted, and turned into the personification of evil and the bane of humanity. I have no desire to join their company.

The realization of all this gave me an entirely new perspective. Instead of feeling as though God was letting me down, I saw that I was letting him down. My attitudes were foul to him. To label my fever of relentless comparisons with as benign a term as the "greener-grass syndrome" grossly missed the naked truth. My healing came when I called my feelings what they were.

7. I find new ways to compare myself with others. Sin finds a way to mutate and in its new form goes unrecognized for a time. When I had largely gotten my previous practice of comparing under control, it took a new shape. Just as parts of the body can become weak and susceptible to infection, so the fever of envy hits where I feel weakest; and now, in my mid-forties, I increasingly feel it with regard to my appearance. I can tick off a half-dozen things about my looks (progressive baldness, for one) that I feel lessen my winsomeness. I don't think much about it until I am around someone with obvious physical advantages and I suddenly have visceral feelings that if verbalized would sound something like "You lucky dog."

Again I am reminded, "What a wretched man I am! Who will rescue me from this body of death? Thanks be to God—through Jesus Christ our Lord!"

Conviction-based ministry

Like lust, wrongful comparisons are a spiritual battle that through Christ I must guard against and defeat, one day at a time. What I long for, and believe I am learning, is a Christ-centered view of ministry based on ten convictions:

1. God is the one who assigns my task (1 Cor. 3:5).
2. God determines the scope of my ministry (2 Cor. 10:13–16).
3. God gives me the gifts he wants me to have (1 Cor. 12:4–11).
4. God is the one who makes me fruitful (1 Cor. 3:6).
5. God opens and closes doors (Col. 4:3).
6. God is the one who lifts people up (Ps. 75:6–7).
7. God bestows positions of high visibility even to the lowliest of people. When God gives great authority to someone, it does not necessarily mean that he approves more of that person or that they are more spiritual or holy than I am (Dan. 4:17).
8. By the grace of God we have our ministries (1 Cor. 3:10).
9. No ministry deserves more credit than another (1 Cor. 3:7).
10. What matters to God is our faithfulness (Matt. 25:14–30).

These beliefs enable me to persevere with contentment in the places God has commissioned me to be.

After a meal of fish on the shore of the Sea of Galilee, when the resurrected Jesus had finished reinstating Peter, he concluded with the simple words "Follow me!" True to form, Peter immediately blundered. He turned to the disciple whom Jesus loved and could not resist comparison.

"Lord, what about him?" Peter asked.

When I have given chores to one of my boys, often the first question out of his mouth is "What about [my brother]?" The motivation for this question is more than a concern for fairness; often I get the strong sense it is merely a diversion, a way of avoiding a command.

I have no patience with that question and usually respond, "Don't worry about him; you do what I said."

This is roughly how Jesus responded to Peter: "If I want him to remain alive until I return," he said, "*What is that to you? You must follow me*" [italics mine].

In other words, what the Lord does with someone else is none of my business. My concern must be with the command of my Lord to me. I cannot allow comparisons with others to distract me from the one thing that truly matters: following Jesus.

8

WHEN THE ROPE UNCLIPS

MY SON MARK HAD PRACTICED gymnastics for several years and he was ready to learn a double back flip on the trampoline. His coach buckled a spotting belt around Mark's waist and clipped on two ropes that stretched upward to two pulleys on ceiling beams some thirty feet apart and then rejoined and dropped back down to the spotter. If Mark was about to fall on his head, the coach would pull on the rope and suspend him in the air. Mark practiced doubles safely for several weeks in the spotting belt and proudly reported to me how well he was doing.

Then one Saturday he came home with bruises on his head and hip and a disquieting story. In the middle of a double flip, when Mark's coach pulled on the ropes, one of them came unclipped from the steel ring on the belt. Since the remaining rope ran to a ceiling pulley many feet to the side of the trampoline, Mark swung pendulum-like sideways off the trampoline, where he met a wall.

Until this episode, Mark had placed complete confidence in the spotting belt. Suddenly he did not know what to expect from it.

The same sort of thing has happened to me a few times in my ministry. Based on my interpretation and application of Scripture, I thought I knew what I could expect from God. Then something came unclipped, and I swung in a direction I did not anticipate, leaving me disillusioned and sometimes pondering whether I should quit.

One of these times came in 1994. After serving as associate editor at LEADERSHIP for three years, I had ventured into free-lance writing and itinerant preaching. Financially, this was an extremely risky move. I could not predict from week to week what my honorariums would be, if any. I paid my own health and life insurance, and I had a wife and four sons to house, feed, and clothe.

But I felt I was within God's will and therefore not presumptuous, and I wanted to bank on God's promise to meet my needs if I sought first his kingdom and his righteousness. I believed God would supply all my needs according to his glorious riches in Christ Jesus; that if I asked, I would receive. I had no illusions that it would be easy but I was convinced God would make a way.

Several months into my new venture, my finances grew leaner and leaner. Preaching honorariums almost always fell far below what I needed. I wrote and mailed out a number of book proposals to publishers, who were not interested. In the meantime I wrote magazine articles, which usually pay at a rate that works out to minimum wage. Gradually I fell further and further behind in my bills.

Lord, I cannot believe you want me behind in my bills, I would pray. *This is not a good witness. I cannot believe you want me to struggle like this, to spend such emotional energy just to meet daily needs.*

Everything came to a head in the summer of 1994. The IRS had hit me with an unexpected tax bill, and we were now several thousand dollars in debt. In desperation, I put this debt on a high-interest credit card. Other bills remained outstanding. I was getting to the point of no return; I had to make some decisions about whether to make a course correction.

As the noose tightened around my neck, I began to flirt with questions I had never before allowed myself to think. Could I depend on God or not? Could I rely on his promises or not? As far as I could see, I was doing all I could: working hard six and seven days a week, praying, seeking first the kingdom through writing and preaching. I checked my motives and felt they were fairly good. In short, things just did not add up.

As I pondered my situation, a terrible feeling of insecurity swept over me, something like a ship captain must feel when his anchor gives way in a storm. The questions I was asking ultimately addressed issues that went beyond merely paying the bills to the very core issues of my faith. If these promises about provision were not reliable, what was? If the Book does not work when it comes to finances, how can I know it will work in regard to other spiritual issues?

Disillusionment sapped my ability to persevere. I had

to preach the Word, and I was wondering how to interpret it! If I was to hang in there with God's work, I had to understand the nature of prayer and God's promises and the difference between faith and presumption. I needed to be able to trust God.

I have found the health of human relationships often revolves around expectations—ours and theirs. If my expectations for my wife do not match reality, I am disappointed. The same holds true in my relationship with God. I cannot put God in a box, but I need to know what I should realistically expect of him. If my expectations are unscriptural, I am living under an illusion and will someday experience a jarring collision with a wall. All the same, just as surely as I did not want to presume upon God, neither did I want to veer to the other extreme of having a small God (to use Phillips' phrase). That, too, is an illusion and one, I suspect, that is more displeasing to the Lord than presumption.

I think by now my bias is clear: if I am going to err, I choose to do so on the side of faith. But I was face-to-face with stark reality. I was in a no-man's-land, where a minister cannot long endure. I could not continue to risk everything while unsure about my beliefs. I had to know what I could expect from God in the future. Had I built my life on false expectations?

Over the next six months as I worked through my finances and my Bible, I learned several things about myself and about God.

1. *Remember to remember.* I quickly forget how God has worked in my life in the past, much as the Israelites forgot how God delivered them from Egypt and led them in the desert. Even though they had repeatedly seen God work mighty wonders on their behalf, with each new peril they complained in full throat that God had left them and that all was lost.

I have read this Exodus account often, with full knowledge of how the story ends, and I have thought, *How can they be so dense! Only days before God parted the Red Sea and they walked through on dry ground. On top of that, they saw God's power on their behalf against the Egyptians. How can they not see that God will help them now as he did before?* Yet when I face troubles far less perilous than the Israelites faced (never have I walked with my children for days through a desert without food and water), I am just as quick to shout, "Woe is me!"

In my times of disillusionment, I find it helpful to remember how God has previously pulled me from the fire. Once when I pastored in Chicago, for example, with my salary in the $22,000 range and bills excruciatingly tight, I had slowly fallen behind some $1,500. One day a friend who knew nothing about my bills gave me a check that covered the majority of them, and soon we were out of the woods. I rejoiced because I had seen God's promises proven true. On another occasion, in winter, the church boiler had burst, and we needed some $6,000 for a new one. Our inner-city church had no money, so I prayed earnestly for God to help us. Within days he provided through neighboring churches that rallied to our aid. Our church worshiped God joyfully for making a way for us.

I can say categorically that God has *never* failed me in

the past. Not once have our cupboards been bare. Not once has my family lacked food, clothing, shelter, or transportation. The Lord has always been faithful and trustworthy.

2. Develop "radical listening" skills. In the middle of my crisis of confidence in the summer of 1994, I decided that at all cost I had to find out what was wrong. I had not discovered it through my reasoning or through talking it out with fellow ministers, so I had to take another tack.

I determined to devote myself to seeking the Lord until he gave me insight into the cause of my circumstances. Of course I had already been praying hard for months, but I had also been under pressure to write as much as possible in order to pay the bills. Now I decided to risk everything on God—to put my work aside and fast, pray, read Scripture, and listen for God's voice. I called it "radical listening" because I was in such desperate straits.

On the first day, after several hours, I felt impressed to read Amos 4. Unsure whether I had "heard" God accurately, I opened the Bible with apprehension, only to have my soul galvanized by the sense that God was apparently at work, for the words seemed directly relevant to my situation. Amos declared God had withheld rain from Israel and struck their crops with plagues because of Israel's sin. God called Israel to return to him.

The parallel was all too clear. My life was marked by drought. I realized that in all likelihood my financial shortfalls had resulted from conduct that was displeasing to the Lord. The clearest area of disobedience was my marriage. My wife and I had not been getting along well—owing first to some issues we had never worked through and second to our financial problems. Furthermore, I had not properly involved her in the process of making my decision to undertake free-lance writing and itinerant preaching. I saw that I was not trying hard enough to hear her concerns and work together toward a solution.

The impression I had from Amos 4 was confirmed twice. To ensure that I had heard properly, I continued for several days to spend devoted time to seeking the Lord. He impressed only two other Scriptures on my heart: Jeremiah 14 and the book of Haggai. Again, my soul was quickened as I read; both passages addressed the subject of lack having been sent by the Lord to wake up his people.

I was certain now that I lacked provision not because God's promise had failed but because I had failed. I took steps to correct the areas of disobedience and slippage, and over several months our financial situation gradually improved as a spate of work came my way and honorariums improved. Within eight months we were in the black.

Paul's word to the Philippians had come true for me: "If on some point you think differently, that too God will make clear to you" (3:15).

3. *Look hard in the mirror.* I have two cars—a 1992 Toyota Corolla and a 1984 Chevy Cavalier. The latter has 135,000 miles on it that are all mine. Naturally I have had to replace many parts on the Chevy over the years, but only recently did I learn that one of the more expensive replacements should have been unnecessary. Several years after I bought the car, I started having problems with the radiator, and around 1992 I replaced it at a cost of several hundred dollars. I blamed Chevy for having a shoddy product.

When I took my Toyota in for maintenance a few years later, however, I learned something about cars. "The most important maintenance," said the service manager, "is to replace the fluids. You need to change your oil every 3,000 miles and flush your radiator every two years." This is because after two years antifreeze undergoes a chemical change and becomes corrosive, ruining the radiator. Throughout the life of my Chevy Cavalier, I had never once flushed the radiator! So I was to blame for the failure, not Chevy.

During my season of disillusionment, I made the same mistake with God. The problem was not God's promises but my disobedience. If I ever again face similar disillusioning circumstances, I am determined to take the attitude that the problem is with me; I am missing something. I am the one with limited perceptions; I am the one who has distortions in understanding because of sin. I am the one who needs to humble myself and accept God's Word as true, even when I cannot make it fit my experience.

I like the way David expresses this attitude in Psalm 131: "My heart is not proud, O Lord, my eyes are not haughty; I do not concern myself with great matters or things too wonderful for me. But I have stilled and quieted my soul; like a weaned child with its mother, like a weaned child is my soul within me. O Israel, put your hope in the Lord both now and forevermore."

Someone has said we become disillusioned when we hold on to an illusion. I believe this was indeed the case with me. Not that anything in God's Word is an illusion, but I always thought I should be able to understand all of God's ways in my life at the very time that they are happening. Therein lay the illusion. In fact, Scripture assures me that much of the time I will *not* understand God's activity!

4. Account for anomalies. Scripture shows that God occasionally works in people's lives in untypical ways. The events that do not fit our current understanding are something like the anomalies of science that for a season puzzle physicists.

For example, when Einstein was a young man, physicists had already scratched their heads for some fifty years over the unexplainable orbit of the planet Mercury. Newton's theories of gravity had served well for centuries to understand the orbits of all the other planets. But in Mercury's elliptical orbit, the point nearest the sun drifted by a very small amount: "5,600 seconds of arc per century," according to Walter Sullivan. "Newton's theory explained all but forty-three seconds of this by taking into account the gravity of other planets."

Astronomers conjectured that another small hidden planet, which they named Vulcan, might orbit near the sun and exert gravitational force on Mercury. But Vulcan was never discovered. Until Einstein came on the scene, those forty-three seconds of arc remained a stubborn anomaly.

But then Einstein formulated his general theory of relativity. When he applied this gravitational formula to the eccentric orbit of Mercury, he experienced one of the breathtaking moments of his scientific life: the numbers fit. Mercury's forty-three seconds were no longer an anomaly.

My life will occasionally take on an orbit like Mercury's that for a time simply defies my best efforts to explain it. Nonetheless, as surely as there is order in the universe, there is a heavenly reason for my circumstances that is utterly consistent with God's Word and character. I simply cannot understand it yet.

The Bible records many circumstances that contradict what I would expect of God:

- God commands Abraham to emigrate to the Promised Land and, once there, the first thing Abraham finds is famine—severe famine. An anomaly.
- God tells Abraham to sacrifice his son. An anomaly.
- David eats the consecrated bread. An anomaly.
- God commands Ezekiel to eat food cooked over human dung. An anomaly.
- God commands Hosea to marry a prostitute. An anomaly.
- Jesus shows mercy to sinners for four years; then when Ananias and Sapphira lie, God strikes them dead. An anomaly.
- Jesus hangs on the cross and cries out, "My God, my God, why have you forsaken me?" An anomaly.

I can trust God's Word, but I cannot lock God into a formula. At the same time, I must take care not to make what seems like an exception into the rule. For example, if I do not see the provision I expect for some period of time, I cannot say God's promises of provision cannot stand the acid test. The rule is the rule, and an apparent exception is precisely that.

I heard one analogy that has helped me. For an airplane to fly, one law of physics must supersede another. The laws of aerodynamics must take precedence over the law of gravity. Airplane flight does not mean that the law of gravity has failed, only that another law has taken precedence. So it is that on occasion one principle of Scripture supplants another. In my case, for example, as it often was for the Israelites, God's discipline superseded his provision.

5. *Wait for time to prove God right.* A few months before my disillusionment hit, I figured out how much money I would need, not only to get out of debt and pay current bills but also to purchase some things we desperately needed and had delayed buying. The amount was $10,000. I began to pray for this specific amount to come in. Extraordinarily. Beyond my regular income.

When nothing happened, I went through my deep disillusionment. As I said before, I entered a period of radical listening; I corrected some things in my life; and after a few months my finances slowly improved, though the week-to-week pressure remained.

About another six months passed. And then one year after I had first prayed for the miraculous supply of

$10,000, I received a completely unforeseen gift from a family member for exactly $10,000. That check took us out of the woods, and since then we have kept pace with our expenses and enjoyed the most pressure-free time in our financial lives.

Situations like this have shown me again and again that time proves God's promises true, often an extensive amount of time. The short run is deceptive.

Through this entire experience, Psalm 89 has taken on special meaning for me. Written by a Jew after the destruction of Jerusalem, this psalm is an account of cognitive dissonance.

Without a hint of his anguish, the psalmist begins with praise to God for his faithfulness and love. He writes at length of the covenant God established with David and quotes God's promise to establish David's line forever even if his sons stray.

Then in a jarring, abrupt reversal in tone, the psalmist addresses God in the second person, recounting in accusatory terms how God has cast David's throne to the ground. "Where is your former great love," he asks, "which in your faithfulness you swore to David?" He begs God to remember Israel and finishes with a curt, almost obligatory "Praise be to the Lord forever! Amen and Amen."

On the one hand, the psalmist knows what God has promised; on the other, history and his experience contradict those promises. He cannot reconcile the two no matter how hard he tries. He believes God's Word, yet he must face a reality that seems to deny God's Word can ever be fulfilled.

From my position in history, though, I know how God's faithful covenant was and is being fulfilled, and, to a degree, that surpasses anything David could have imagined. God himself would become David's royal descendant and establish an eternal kingdom of absolute justice and righteousness that would fill the universe. Despite how unlikely it appeared to the psalmist, God is fulfilling his covenant to David.

David—and Moses and Abraham and Joseph and Esther and Ruth and Mary, among many others—teaches me that when God's promises appear the least likely to be fulfilled, he is working out ambitious projects that dwarf my capacity even to conceive of them.

My problem is that I live in a fax-machine culture. If my computer takes a half-second to obey a command, I want to spend thousands of dollars to upgrade. My culture conditions me to expect everything quickly. If I bring those expectations to God, however, I am usually disappointed. God is the Timeless One, for whom a thousand years are as a day. He knows most of his highest purposes for me are realized in a time-intensive process, so he uses Old Man Time as a chisel on my inner man.

And so in my times of disillusionment I have learned to simply persevere no matter what circumstances or thoughts buzz around me. My mind may never resolve every question, but time will.

I must not put an arbitrary statute of limitations on God's Word. If I become disillusioned again, it will be a failure of my patience, not of God's promise. He encourages me in almost unqualified terms to pray and believe but he reserves to himself the date of fulfillment.

6. *Focus on what God pursues.* My faith, like my character, is an end in itself, not merely a means by which God gives me what I ask. Christ is the author and perfecter of my faith. I expect, then, that God will allow circumstances that demand faith, hence circumstances that by definition defy my reasoning and expectations, that force me to trust in spite of everything. Because faith is the goal, I should expect God to defy my expectations.

After my son Mark's accident on the trampoline, the owner of the gymnastics club took action to ensure that such a mishap would not occur again. He installed a safety latch to keep the clip from accidentally unclipping. God is likewise interested in my safety. If I will do the one thing he clearly instructs me to do—persevere—he will ultimately show himself faithful. In the long run, God is always found true.

9

FAITH FOR THE LOW-YIELD YEARS

AT TIMES I HAVE FELT that my work in ministry was wasted. My prayers did not appear to be answered. My sermons did not seem to change lives. My counseling did not appear to help people. My evangelism won no converts. My leadership initiatives were ignored. My discipling of others seemed to bring no growth. Even in the areas of my strongest gifting, my efforts have occasionally looked utterly ineffective.

At such times I identify with the apparent contradiction described in Isaiah 49:1–4. There God speaks of his high purpose for his people, comparing them to a sharpened sword and a polished arrow for divine use. "You are my servant, Israel," the Lord concludes, "in whom I will display my splendor."

But the servant of the Lord has quite a different feeling. "I have labored to no purpose," he replies. "I have spent my strength in vain and for nothing. Yet what is due me is in the Lord's hand, and my reward is with my God." In apparent futility, the servant can only console himself with his ultimate reward from God.

Most who have ministered in churches for any length of time have known the servant's paradoxical state: a stirring sense of call and a frequent sense of futility. We do the most important work in the world with the greatest resources imaginable, yet we sometimes feel as though we are accomplishing nothing. What gives?

As I have mulled over this paradox for several decades, I have come to some conclusions that help me to persevere with peace of mind even when tangible results are few and far between.

1. *I can influence but I cannot control.* Spiritual work has limits. The nature of these limits is illustrated by the difference between the work of a farmer and that of a cabinetmaker.

With tools like saws and routers, a cabinetmaker directly and immediately molds his product to conform to his vision. There is no delay between the push of the circular saw and the cut of the board, and if he pushes the saw to the left, it goes to the left. If he wants a half-inch-wide groove along the lower edge of the board, he uses a router or chisel to make one. Because the tools and wood have no life or will of their own, the results of the cabinetmaker's work are primarily a function of his skill and diligence. In other words, a cabinetmaker enjoys almost complete control.

A farmer, on the other hand, has influence but no real control. He works in partnership with a host of other forces, resources, and living things: soil, sun, seed, weather, pests, fertilizer, and, ultimately, God. A farmer works indirectly with his crop, encouraging an environment for growth with fertilizer, weeding, and irrigation. Because he deals with living things, a farmer cannot directly shape his crops. And because living things require time to grow, a farmer must wait patiently for the process to be completed.

Jesus repeatedly used the farming analogy for good reason. Even he did not force people into the kingdom but only influenced them. I can pray for others, love them, teach them, challenge them, but I cannot make decisions for them.

In recent weeks I have been on-again-off-again frustrated with someone whom I am trying to help get on his feet as a Christian. He says he has committed his life to Christ but in six months has attended church only a few times and resists my efforts to disciple him one-on-one. He will not return my phone calls. When I do catch him at home, he says he is too busy to study the Bible together over the phone. A tentative appointment to talk yesterday went by the wayside. Last night, in frustration, I thought to myself, *I'm going to quit pursuing him; I'll pray for him but I'm going to wait for him to come to us.*

No, I cannot do that, I told myself later. *He is a baby Christian who needs a shepherd.* His resistance should not surprise me, considering his life prior to his conversion. The truth is, I am frustrated—largely because I want control. I want A plus B to quickly equal C. I want to be able to employ techniques that yield results as directly as the cause-and-effect world of the cabinetmaker.

2. *Any growth in righteousness is of infinite value.* In the 1996 Summer Olympics, sprinter Michael Johnson set records in the 200- and 400-meter races. To do so he trained for some ten years to cut a mere second or two from his time. In *Slaying the Dragon* he writes,

> Success is found in much smaller portions than most people realize. A hundredth of a second here or sometimes a tenth there can determine the fastest man in the world. At times we live our lives on a paper-thin edge that barely separates greatness from mediocrity and success from failure.[1]

Few people would suggest Michael Johnson had trained in vain, yet he toiled for a mere medal and title—passing glories. How much more valuable is the hard work pastors invest in others to produce even "small" gains in obedience to the will of God.

In fact, there is no such thing as *minor* repentance. Granted, in this fallen world, to help one person overcome a sinful habit, such as a critical spirit, can seem about as productive as cleaning one piece of gum from the sidewalk of a trash-laden ghetto. But to God, who is infinitely into the details, all righteousness matters, every effort counts.

Therefore, all my discipling matters immensely. For example, if I preach to forty people and only one righteous deed results in the life of one person—a mother, perhaps, resists the temptation to lose her temper with her child—it is of eternal significance. Any conformity to

---

[1]Michael Johnson, *Slaying the Dragon* (New York: Harper-Collins, 1996).

the will of God is of infinite worth. If *one* sin—a bite from the forbidden fruit—could be so cataclysmic as to send Christ to the cross, then it is worth preventing even one sin. If *one* act of righteousness—Mary's anointing of the body of Jesus—could lead to her story being told wherever the gospel is preached, then one act of obedience is of immense worth. If at the last judgment *every* careless word will be brought to account, *every* motive judged, and *every* good deed receive its reward, then *everything* in the realm of human conduct matters. In God's eyes, the vileness of one sin or the eternal glory of one righteous act exceeds anything we can imagine.

Paul knew this, and this knowledge was the engine of his pastoral work. "We proclaim him," he said, "admonishing and teaching everyone with all wisdom, so that we may present everyone perfect in Christ. To this end I labor, struggling with all his energy, which so powerfully works in me" (Col. 1:28). These words are not merely the Pharisaical personality distortion of an obsessive-compulsive perfectionist, but rather a true reflection of the value of each bit of repentance and growth in any person. Clearly Paul expresses the mind of Christ, who said, "Go and make disciples of all nations . . . teaching them to obey *everything* I have commanded you" (Matt. 28:19–20, emphasis mine).

What people do and think and say matter so much that to spend our entire lives on the growth of only one person is worthwhile, not in a fastidious spirit of Pharisaical legalism but in the freedom of those who have a joyful desire to please the one who loves righteousness.

Given this truth, I know I actually see few of the true

results of my ministry, for I cannot follow people around in their daily lives to see how God is gradually changing them. After I preach, people walk away and their lives are changed in ways I cannot know now, but one day I will see it. Then I will realize that the results of my work far exceed the winning of even a hundred Olympic gold medals. I will know for a certainty that righteousness is real—that it has eternal significance.

3. Ministry is measured in many ways. A year ago I received an evaluation form in the mail from my denominational superiors to be used in the annual review of my ministry at our church. The form asked for data on attendance, income, missions giving, and one or two other numerical criteria for the previous three years. After I completed the form, it seemed to me that the report did not tell the whole story, for by its measure little had happened during the previous year. And that was not the case, for in many critical intangibles good things were happening.

For this reason, I added an additional sheet in which I rated the strength of our church on a scale of one to ten in areas I felt were critical, such as the quality of our worship and our relationships, progress on our vision, our effectiveness in evangelism, our spirit of giving, the degree to which members responded to my leadership, the levels of unity, joy, faith, and morale among the congregation.

This was not merely an attempt to put a positive spin on a lackluster report. On some of the added criteria we fared well and on others poorly, but I felt the new-and-improved evaluation better pictured what was actually happening. By these measures, we were seeing results, the kind that I trust will eventually lead to tangible fruit.

4. Spiritual ministry requires faith from beginning to end. Salvation is not the only thing in the Christian life that depends on faith; so does Christian ministry. "We continually remember before our God and Father," said Paul, "your work produced by faith" (1 Thess. 1:3). God delights in our faith too much to let ministry be based primarily on works. Consequently, if I am following his leading, I find that he often orders my ministry in the church in a way that requires my faith.

In practical terms, this means I often have less security and control than I would prefer. When fears arise and I wonder if God is really with me, I remind myself that on this earth kingdom ministry never graduates to a point where I no longer need faith.

This fact has huge implications for those concerned about results. I must see my faith as an end in itself, valuable in itself, a fruit of ministry as valid as conversions or numerical growth. All Job did was believe, in spite of everything, yet he pleased God greatly. Some pastors must plant themselves in a community—like Abraham in the Promised Land—and pray and believe for a season without tangible results because God delights in their faith in the same way he delighted in Abraham's faith (which waited a long time before seeing results!). Like Paul, who delighted in hardships because Christ's power rested on him at those times, I am learning to delight in situations that require faith, for then I know my heart pleases God.

If God wants to bear the fruit of hundreds of conversions through me, I will thank him for it. If God wants to produce faith in me in the face of few tangible results, I will believe him for the coming of his kingdom in people's lives—sooner, or later.

Naturally there is an aberration of this kind of faith. Faith must not become a rationale for laziness or passivity, a failure to do my part in the divine-human partnership called ministry. I am careful to prayerfully think through the ministries of our church to be sure we have biblical purposes and effective strategies to fulfill them.

5. *Spiritual seeds have enduring power.* On September 6, 1622, the Spanish galleon *Atocha*, bristling with bronze cannons and laden with gold and silver, served as the rear guard of a twenty-eight vessel flotilla in the Gulf of Mexico. A hurricane struck, and the *Atocha* sank near the Marquesas Keys of the Florida coast, where it remained for 365 years.

In the 1980s a treasure hunter and a college professor who had pored over Spanish documents of the voyage found the *Atocha*. Among those who examined the boat's contents was an archaeologist, and in the sand that had served as its ballast he found something of special interest: seeds. To keep them from drying out he put the seeds in cups of fresh water. Nine days later as he checked the water level in the cups, he made a surprising discovery: "Suddenly, I saw leaves sticking up," he says. To his astonishment, four of the seeds had sprouted.

As this account verifies, the seeds of this natural world are miracles endued by God with the power of life.

Can the seeds of the spiritual world be any less powerful? Indeed, they have greater staying power.

In an important parable about seeds that gets less attention than the familiar parable of the four soils, Jesus described this power:

> This is what the kingdom of God is like. A man scatters seed on the ground. Night and day, whether he sleeps or gets up, the seed sprouts and grows, though he does not know how. All by itself the soil produces grain—first the stalk, then the head, then the full kernel in the head. (Mark 4:26–28)

God's Word has power long after we sow it. Ideas, principles, beliefs, and insights based on Scripture have staying power. While the soil may be hostile to their growth now, while birds may carry some seeds away, in many people the seeds will someday germinate and take root. Because I believe in the enduring power in the seeds of truth, I can endure even in the seasons when I see little or no results.

Several months ago the church in Chicago where I previously served as pastor asked me to preach on a Sunday night. Because ten years had passed since my ministry there I did not expect to see many familiar faces. At the church dinner before the meeting, however, I found otherwise. The room was filled with people whom I knew well. My greatest surprise—and joy—was to see many people who had not been regulars of the church during my time: non-Christians whom we had tried to bring to Christ or immature believers struggling to escape the allure of the world. While some were still in-and-out, others had become regular churchgoers and church workers with Christian families.

I was especially gratified to see one young man. During my time in the pastorate, he had not attended with his mother; and in the months before my resignation, he had fallen into gang trouble and been locked away in prison. I had visited him at the Cook County jail and encouraged him to reach out to the Lord and trust in Christ for salvation. I also visited his wife, who started coming to church irregularly. Eventually he went to the penitentiary. But he had served his time, and I saw him at the church dinner with his wife and young children—a family man and a believer in Jesus Christ.

I was deeply moved with a sense that my ministry with the people in this church had mattered greatly. Now, with a long-term perspective, I saw more results from my ministry than I had seen before. The seeds of truth and love keep working long after they are sown. There is no way around it; spiritual ministry takes time.

The evening at my old church encouraged me to continue the simple method of the apostle Paul: "By setting forth the truth plainly," he said, "we commend ourselves to every man's conscience in the sight of God" (2 Cor. 4:2). In other words, sow the seeds and patiently, prayerfully watch God work on a person's conscience. This holds true not only in evangelism but in discipleship and church leadership. My responsibility is simply to love people, present the truth, give understanding, appeal to people to move into God's will, pray for them—and watch the kingdom come. Sooner or later the results

God intends will spring forth.

6. *Each step people make in God's direction should be celebrated.* Our church worships in the second-floor conference room of the IBM building in downtown Chicago, overlooking the Chicago River. During the summer months, we see through the full-length windows the raising of the cantilever bridges, which work like a pair of opposing drawbridges to allow sailboats to pass on their way to Lake Michigan. Any boat coming from the south branch of the river must pass through a bridge nearly every block—some ten of them.

The city does not stop traffic for stray boats, nor do they raise all the bridges at once. Doing so would almost completely cut off automobile traffic into the Loop from the north and west. Instead, one bridge is raised at a time while a cluster of six to eight sailboats passes through. These wait, then, for the next bridge to rise. Step by step the boats eventually reach beautiful Lake Michigan.

Like these sailboats, individuals usually move closer to the Lord one commitment at a time, and the church moves toward greater fruitfulness one step at a time. If I save my sense of satisfaction until the ultimate goal is reached, I will be a frustrated man. I have learned instead to celebrate every bridge we pass through.

Several weeks ago, for instance, I rejoiced with the leaders of our small groups at the progress of a well-educated young man. When he first came to our church, he was emotionally distraught over a divorce and attended our meetings regularly for a few weeks until his feet were back on the ground. But then his attendance trailed off, and we would see him at a worship service only once every few months. We encouraged him to join a small group and he tried this, but soon he became irregular there, as well. It seemed he would never get on track.

But then about two months ago things suddenly changed. He started attending his small group regularly and has attended Sunday worship several times. When I talk to him, I get the feeling his faith is taking hold, that he is stabilizing. He still has a long way to go, but he has passed through a bridge or two, and we are celebrating.

7. *Spiritual ministry is a mixture of muddle and glory.* I enjoy watching most sports, but above all I enjoy playoff hockey. Sometimes I wonder why I do, because most of the game is a muddle of misplays. Rarely do players make more than three consecutive passes before their team loses the puck because of a bad pass, poor stick-handling, a steal, or a check from an opposing player. One team has the puck for a few seconds, and then the other. When a player does come free to shoot at the goal, the goalie almost always stops it. If I were looking for results—goals scored—90 percent of the time a hockey game is an exercise in futility. But now and then, like the sun briefly piercing through the clouds on an overcast day, out of the muddle something right suddenly happens for the offensive team. In the blink of an eye, someone makes a brilliant pass and an offensive player comes open with the puck in front of the goalie. He lets fly, and the puck sinks into the net. The players celebrate as if they had just entered heaven itself.

In my experience, pastoral ministry is like this. Like

hockey, ministry does not appear to be a thing of order and well-scripted results (like football) but rather of mistakes and frustration. There is a lot of muddle. Occasionally, though, I see moments of glory so joyful they make the muddle worthwhile. Someone commits his or her life to Christ. A marriage is saved. Someone becomes a truly sacrificing servant of the church. The purpose of it all is realized.

Why do I like hockey so much? Perhaps because I played on frozen creeks as a kid and took frozen pucks off my shins; perhaps because I grew up loving the Chicago Blackhawks, in awe of their star Bobby Hull. But it may be, too, that I am wired by God to enjoy something that requires persevering through much grind and seeming futility to know those occasional moments of overwhelming, euphoric joy. In short, I am called to ministry.

In "Total Eclipse" Annie Dillard writes,

> The Ring Nebula, in the constellation Lyra, looks, through binoculars, like a smoke ring. It is a star in the process of exploding. Light from its explosion first reached the earth in 1054; it was a supernova then, and so bright it shone in the daytime. Now it is not so bright but it is still exploding. It expands at the rate of seventy million miles a day. It is interesting to look through binoculars at something expanding at this rate: it does not budge. Its apparent size does not increase. Photographs of the Ring Nebula taken fifteen years ago *seem* identical to photographs taken of it yesterday.[2]

---

[2]Annie Dillard, "Total Eclipse," *The Annie Dillard Reader* (New York: Harper-Collins, 1994), 11–12.

The Ring Nebula teaches us that huge happenings are not always apparent to the naked eye, and that is especially true in the spiritual realm. If I could see from heaven's perspective, I would know that in the spiritual realm when progress appears slowest, kingdom movement is actually occurring—perhaps even at the rate of seventy million miles a day.

10

LOSING MY APPETITE FOR CYNICISM

SEVERAL YEARS AGO, through a series of bad experiences, I developed for a short time a quirky, negative attitude toward banks.

At the time, I ministered and provided for my family through free-lance writing and itinerant speaking, and we endured a long period of financial pressure. Any unexpected expense was a blow, and over a period of a month or two, several of those blows came from the bank. With no margin in our checking account, we made a recording error, writing a large check and not entering it in the register. Before we knew it, four checks had bounced, and for each one the bank charged an NSF fee of twenty dollars—eighty dollars in all!

Other things happened that compounded the pressure I felt.

I deposited a check from someone that later came back unpaid, and the bank charged me an extra fee for that person's NSF check. In the local news at the time, a bank in Chicago incurred a public relations fiasco by announcing their intention to charge three dollars each time a customer used a human teller instead of the ATM machine. To me, it seemed banks were suddenly becoming predators.

I was under pressure and my emotions spilled over one day at a convenient target. "Banks are leeches," I said to my wife when I received one of the fee notices.

Sounds pretty irrational, but nevertheless I did not withdraw my vast fortune and stuff it under the mattress. And my sanity returned to where I understood that banks are a business with the same profit motive as any other business.

I admit this bit of foolishness in order to show you something about myself: under certain circumstances my thinking can become distorted. If I am under enough pressure and others inflict enough pain on me, I can become cynical.

Such was the case, as outlined in chapter 5, when some ten people rose up in opposition to my leadership and within six months our church declined in attendance by 40 percent. I had never before faced church people who seemed deliberately out to get me. Nor had I ever worked with people who assumed the worst about one another's motives and as a result grossly misunderstood the actions and words of others.

On one occasion, for instance, a leader of one of our children's ministries asked if the church would purchase Bibles and present one to each child as a gift. I said I thought it was a great idea but that the money should come out of the children's ministry fund, not the general fund. I found out later that I was heavily criticized for this decision and cast as a pastor who was unconcerned about getting Bibles into the hands of our young people.

The whole experience was frightening and disillusioning, and it caught me completely by surprise. Frankly, I naïvely thought I was above such opposition. I believed my motives were right and I was doing my best, and consequently everyone should and would think highly of me. With deep sadness, I learned through this experience that no one is above conflict.

The incident threw my assumptions about life out of kilter. Those who "betrayed" me in this were leaders whom I had trusted, to whom I had given responsibility, and to whom I had been vulnerable. I had sought their good and not their harm. If I could not trust these people, whom could I trust? And so, though I continued to work in the church with determination, in subtle ways I grew pessimistic about people and relationships.

My low-grade pessimism expressed itself in various ways. One symptom was a suspicious attitude toward newcomers to the church. Whereas before I would rejoice over visitors and the possibility of their making our church their home, now I was somewhat wary of them, cautiously wondering who among them would turn on me down the road. And though I had at one time rejected the idea that pastors cannot get close to their people, now I was becoming resigned to it. When I was discouraged, little asides slipped out from my mouth unbidden, such as, "People are impossible." But because cynicism is incompatible with pastoring I never really owned up to that jaded word.

For pastors, even low-grade cynicism can't help but lead to despair, for the ministry is people work. A distrusting pastor is like a cabinetmaker who grows to dislike wood, or an artist who begins to hate to work with paint. I don't know of any pastor who entered the ministry expecting to feel like an American CIA agent in cold-war Moscow. It is natural that cynicism soon leads to a fainthearted desire to quit. Perseverance depends on hope.

Cynicism is not the automatic result of wounds suffered when relationships go wrong. Several of my own attitudes and beliefs provided fertile ground for the choking weeds of distrust.

Favorable environment

The most obvious and morally neutral reason for my cynicism was self-defense. To protect myself and my family from being hurt again, I tried to determine what I could expect from others in this newly dangerous church world, readjusting what I perceived as reality. I wanted to have life and people figured out, predictable (and therefore somewhat controllable).

With a car door, for example, I understand how I could be hurt by one if my hand is in the wrong place at the wrong time: I could smash a few fingers. I know what to expect from a slammed car door. I want the same predictability with people. I don't want any painful surprises. Therefore, it figures that if I treat people as though they are potentially dangerous, I will not be surprised by anyone.

At a deeper level, I now see that I was trying to soften my mistakes, to lessen the degree of my guilt. (I don't want to paint myself too darkly, though, because I tend to be self-critical and follow the maxim that if something is wrong I have somehow contributed to the problem and need to grow through the experience.) The truth is, I was convinced I was easy to work with because I was approachable and easygoing. What I did not want to admit was that in many ways I am in fact difficult to work with. I dislike administrative duties. I avoid policies, procedures, job descriptions. I don't rush to give structure and discipline to the organization. I make decisions slowly, but I love to be spontaneous. This makes things easier for me but difficult for others.

The darkest impulse within my pessimistic heart during this time, however, was subterranean anger, the inevitable fruit of pain, though again I did not recognize my anger as such because I wasn't sitting around nursing malicious thoughts. I felt that my detractors had thoroughly ruined my dreams, caused my hard work to go up in smoke, and deepened my financial pressures. I consciously forgave these people, though, and was careful to speak to others about them with goodwill, even if cold currents of disappointment flowed through me like an icy river in my veins. I could not think about some people who had hurt us without having negative feelings.

Frankly, I found some satisfaction in cynicism. I think it is the warped pleasure of being wise in my own eyes. I wonder if a tinge of cynicism is not a common syndrome of those in their thirties. My youthful hand of idealism had gotten burned a few times, and then my eyes were opened and I thought I had everyone figured out: I knew their real motives. I knew what they might do someday, and I was not going to get snookered again. *I am smarter than that. I am wise to you.*

The most noble reason for my cynicism, however, was idealism. Someone has said that in the breast of every cynic beats the heart of an idealist. That observation indeed describes me. I believe the church can be a glorious community of Christlike people marked by unselfish love. I believe the fellowship of other Christians can be one of the great joys in one's life. I believe the church is the hope of the world. So when my ideals fell in pieces to the ground, my disappointment was overwhelming. Overwrought emotions drove the pendulum of my once-soaring expectations to the opposite extreme—far past a realistic appraisal of human weakness. Cynicism is the mushroom cloud of exploded ideals.

That is why even pastors can be vulnerable to cynicism. We love people, follow stellar ideals fueled by Scripture, and have lofty expectations based on prayer and faith. We are true believers but we have tricky emotions.

The strength of a pastor's negative reaction to the failings of his or her people can also arise from the closeness of the relationship, like a father with a prodigal son. The father believes in his son and wants him to be great. When his son goes astray, others assure the father, "He's just going through a phase. Don't worry. He's a good kid; he'll come out of it." But these thoughts are not in the father's heart, for this relationship cuts too close to the bone. The father is angry, disappointed, and ashamed beyond sound reason. The father cannot believe that his son, his own flesh and blood, the one to whom he has given sound guidance and constant love, could do what he is doing. He might even feel mercy toward someone else's son in the same predicament, but not toward his own.

The bane of cynicism is that it becomes a self-fulfilling prophecy: breeding just what it expects. Distrust spawns distrust. If you don't trust me, I wonder what *your* problem is. For the pessimistic pastor, relationships become harder and harder.

Higher ground

For about two years I did not view cynicism as displeasing to God or offensive to others. But several influences came together to expose it for what it truly is, and I gladly came out from under its malignant shadow.

First of all, I gradually came to understand that due largely to the undertow of my emotions I had believed a lie. A cynical outlook does not conform to reality. Cynicism distorts my outlook by universalizing a few situations or persons. For example, if one person or five or fifty hurt me, I conclude that all of them will hurt me. One board is manipulative, and I assume all are that way. In effect, cynicism is prejudice—a prejudgment that others are untrustworthy before I even know anything about them. The cynic glosses over those who are kind and true.

Rarely do I make the same universalizing error in judgment about other things: because I am caught in a traffic jam on the expressway doesn't mean I will always be caught in one, or if I buy a bag of apples and one of them is rotten, that doesn't mean every bag I buy will contain a rotten apple. Normally I know this. (The more pain involved, however, the more likely will be the misjudgment.) Intense pain caused me to lose my sense of reality with people.

The second thing I learned about my cynicism is especially embarrassing to admit. With the added perspective of time, I came to see my response to some of the people in Arlington Heights as childishly naïve. I had acted like a kindergarten boy at the playground who expected everyone to be nice to him if he was nice to them. When a bully hit me with a rock, I bravely kept on playing, but inside I was sitting on the ground with my lower lip sticking out. It was time to grow up.

Thirdly, one day while reading the Bible I happened across 1 Corinthians 13:7 and its significance did not escape me. "[Love] always protects, *always trusts, always hopes*, always perseveres" (emphasis added). *That cannot be what the Bible means*, I thought. *Obviously I cannot always trust or hope the best of some people. There are bullies in the world!*

But I now realize that to some extent mature love demands that I go into ministry with my eyes open and take the risk. Love is not naïve, but it is not overly self-protective either. Love looks for the good in others, not the bad.

Paul wrote his words about a love that always hopes and trusts to the very Corinthians who had hurt him deeply. Many had spoken contemptuously against him and rejected his authority. Nevertheless, Paul could write,

"I will very gladly spend for you everything I have and expend myself as well. If I love you more, will you love me less?" (2 Cor. 12:15). While the natural response to those who hurt us is to build walls against them, Paul writes, "We have spoken freely to you, Corinthians, and opened wide our hearts to you. We are not withholding our affection from you" (2 Cor. 6:11–12). Seemingly against all evidence to the contrary, he could even say, "I have great confidence in you" (2 Cor. 7:4). Paul followed his own directions to the letter.

If I am optimistic and realistic about relationships (that is, loving and truthful), I recognize the possibility that others may return bad for good, but I am willing to take that pain for the sake of bringing Christ's best to them.

Magazine articles also helped me to see cynicism and hope for what they are. For some time I regarded magazines such as *Guideposts* as Pollyannish. On the other hand, magazines like *Time* had a gritty, negative edge that I enjoyed. But as time passed, I grew tired of all the unremitting bad news and negative perspectives. Cynical journalism caused me to despair, and it certainly was not painting the whole picture. Gradually, seeing cynicism as gloomy and unhealthy, I lost my appetite for it. I wanted to read things that face reality but at the same time are redemptive, and choose to hope.

I remember the first time I heard the word *redemptive* and thought of it as something other than a theological term for salvation. It should be the Christian approach to life. As a group of editors, we were weighing the merits of a particular manuscript that told of one pastor's dark experience. Marshall Shelley, editor at LEADERSHIP, asked how the writer could add something redemptive to the story. His question hit me like a lightning bolt as I realized its significance for my current pessimism about people.

Our gospel is all about redemption, I realized. This includes the redemption of people and churches who bruise pastors. God takes people in the grip of evil and turns the situation around for good.

Redemption is a crucial concept for the healing of a cynic. Redemption looks straight and hard at the evil in the world and the capacity for sin in humanity, yet does not give up. Redemption takes hold of fallen humanity and restores it to the glorious state God intended. Our God is our Redeemer. He brings good out of evil and takes hope to the darkest corners of this world.

Another eye opener for me was an anecdote in an editorial by David Neff in *Christianity Today*.[1] "About five years ago," Neff writes, "Christian social critic Richard John Neuhaus was being driven from the Pittsburgh airport to a speaking engagement. During the drive, one of his hosts persisted in decrying the disintegration of the American social fabric and the disappearance of Christian values from our culture. Cases in point were too numerous to mention, but Pastor Neuhaus's host tried anyway. After the tedious drive, Neuhaus offered these words of advice: 'The times may be bad, but they are the only times we are given. Remember, hope is still a Christian virtue, and despair is a mortal sin.'"

---

[1] *Christianity Today* (April 3, 1995): 24.

That was a paradigm I had not considered. *Cynicism* should be respelled s-i-n-i-c-i-s-m, and like all sin it takes a terrible toll, especially on pastors.

Warped but glorious

Out on itinerant speaking assignments, I talked over Sunday lunch with more than one pastor who was smarting from what church people had done to them, and I saw how their pain had poisoned their attitudes toward people and toward ministry overall. I saw myself in them and realized I didn't want to be like that.

I thought about my father, an attorney, who in the pursuit of justice has seen the nasty side of others on plenty of occasions, yet he remains a positive, joyful person. I realized that his outlook on life must be the result of a conscious choice.

A pastor friend caught my attention one day as we talked about the ministry. He said, "I don't have trouble working with people. That's the easy part of ministry." At that I did a double take; I didn't think anyone could feel that way!

His comment confirmed something to me that is obvious but not quickly accepted by someone like myself. Relational and administrative skills have much to do with how others respond to a leader. Some of my troubles in Arlington Heights were due not only to the faults of others but also to my own. And I have a fair share of them. One weakness I have that ironically multiplies problems with others is a great reluctance to confront. By temperament I seek consensus, peace, and good feelings among people. In the past I have rarely confronted anyone. What this neglect does is delay and aggravate many relational and organizational problems. I am finding that as I practice confrontation, when necessary, in most cases I am drawn closer to others.

For example, one of our church leaders was beginning to slip in Sunday attendance, and then he missed a leaders' meeting without informing me beforehand. Later when I saw him, he said nothing about having missed the meeting. Finally one night I talked to him about the problem, and with a mature attitude he admitted his fault and apologized. We ended that meeting more closely knit in understanding and love than we were before.

As I work on my relationship and leadership skills, I find that I am edging toward the feeling of my pastor friend who said he had no trouble working with people. I feel I am getting somewhat of a grip on how people and organizations work. I thoroughly enjoy the process of church ministry and delight in people who call themselves Christians.

Albeit an irregular hobby, I enjoy woodworking. I find pleasure in the sweet smell of wood, especially when it is cut with the saw. I like sanding wood and feeling its smooth texture, and I appreciate the difference in color, grain, and hardness of the various woods, such as the contrast between pine and cherry. With no small satisfaction, I watch wood slowly take shape into useful things.

Of course I get the stubborn splinter on occasion. Knots as hard as rocks sometimes prevent me from sawing a board as I would like. Sometimes the only boards at the lumberyard are a bit warped, and begrudgingly I make the best of them. On occasion I err with pencil and ruler or drill. Woodworking has its downsides, but I am not put off.

Oscar Wilde says a cynic is someone who knows the price of everything and the value of nothing. A cynic knows everything about barbed splinters, bruised fingers, pinched skin, warped boards. A pastor sees a "carved" parishioner that sooner or later reflects the glory of Jesus Christ.

11

WORKING THE EDGES

"THE TWO FOES OF HUMAN HAPPINESS," says philosopher Arthur Schopenauer, "are pain and boredom."

Boredom, stagnation, restlessness—these are less acute than pain, surely, but they do rob pastors of joy and fulfillment. Even something as stimulating as marital sex can become boring when it is routine, and something as demanding as preaching or as challenging as leadership can grow stale over time.

When this happens, we are in danger.

According to the *Chicago Tribune*, on Father's Day 1997 Ricardo Enamorado set out on a jet ski from Chicago's Wilson Avenue boat ramp and headed north along the shoreline of Lake Michigan. After traveling several miles, at about three in the afternoon he turned around to head back south when the engine on the jet ski suddenly quit. Unable to restart it, he floated along nonchalantly, expecting help to come quickly on the busy waters. Gradually, though, the wind and waves pushed Enamorado farther and farther from shore, and help did not come. By dusk he was frantic. Dressed only in cut-offs, tennis shoes, and a life vest, he spent the night on the chilly waters of the lake.

The next day Coast Guard helicopters and a Chicago fire department chopper equipped with special radar began searching for the lost man. By the end of the day they still had not found him, and Enamorado, hungry and sunburned, spent another night on the dark waters of Lake Michigan.

Finally the next morning one member of the search-and-rescue team spotted a flash of light. Enamorado was signaling in their direction with a mirror. The nearly two-day ordeal was over.

Pastors, too, can lose power and begin to drift. At first it may not seem like any big deal. Things will pick up; something will come along that will revive our work. We may busy ourselves with outside interests. We may even ponder resigning our church and finding another that will show greater appreciation. We may quit giving our best in sermon preparation. We may cut back on the work no one sees, such as extra reading and spiritual disciplines. We may stop believing that God will do something significant through us and our church.

Boredom truly is the subtle, sworn enemy of faithful perseverance. It can be deadly.

Sincere, but sincerely wrong

We have all heard the sincerely given advice proffered to those who are dead in the water and sensed perhaps that solutions like the following can come up short:

1. *"Just be faithful."* Certainly I can always be motivated by my commitment to be faithful to God-given responsibilities, but what confuses me is when faithfulness leads to stagnation. Surely God does not want me or the church to be stagnant. Is long-term boredom, therefore, a sign that I need to initiate a change, that God is leading me elsewhere? How can I be both faithful and challenged?

Another issue brings the facile appeal to faithfulness into question. Boredom often strikes when little is happening in my ministry. When this is the case, I don't want to make the mistake of lingering in ineffectiveness in the name of faithfulness. If I persist at a stalled ministry without a clear sense that God has a purpose for me there, I am doing no one—least of all the Lord—any favors. Perhaps languor signals that I am missing the will of God. "Faithfulness" can even be a way to rationalize complacency, laziness, or outright negligence.

2. *"Keep growing."* Some would say that if I feel bored I need to stretch myself intellectually and sharpen my ministry skills. Pursue a graduate degree; develop hobbies and interests outside the church; cultivate more friendships.

The disquieting thing about this solution is that I could find it in *Dear Abby*. While stagnation likely has some natural as well as spiritual roots, I am not satisfied unless the primary answer is distinctively Christian. What is the spiritual core of boredom and stagnation?

What would Jesus say about it?

And then, of course, there is the pragmatic question: What if you lack the motivation to even pursue the things that will renew your motivation? Catch–22! Or what do you do when you have tried the tried-and-true paths to lifetime growth but your head is still nodding from boredom?

3. *"Pray and read your Bible more."* This is the pill I prescribe to others for almost every ill, and it usually does the trick. Still, as many lament, what do you do when the spiritual disciplines are the most stagnant part of your life?

4. *"Persevere."* Just keep putting one foot in front of the other, no matter how you feel. Duty, will power, determination!

While the Bible does call for perseverance, it does not allow for *hollow* perseverance. One oft-quoted word on the subject says, "Let us not become weary in doing good" (Gal. 6:9). This suggests I should not keep plowing ahead regardless of how I feel, but that I must not even allow the feeling of weariness to linger! I must not continue indefinitely with an engineless perseverance; rather, my heart must be in this. As Romans 12:11 says, "Never be lacking in zeal, but keep your spiritual fervor, serving the Lord."

The appeal of Galatians 6:9 to the will implies personal responsibility for weariness. What choices am I making that have brought me to this enervated place? What will enable me to power up again?

Energizing approaches

In my experience, five frames of mind have proven to keep me stretched and interested in ministry to the fullest.

1. *Maintain internal faithfulness.* Restlessness in ministry and in marriage look alike, and so does the answer to the problem. Malachi said, "Guard yourself in your spirit, and do not break faith with the wife of your youth" (2:15). The key to marital faithfulness is to guard the center of my being: my spirit. If I am faithful in spirit—choosing to delight in my wife in my thoughts—I will avoid the hollow core of boredom that causes me restlessly to turn my attention to other women.

Mere external faithfulness is an attempt to stay true in conduct even though I break faith in my heart, and it inevitably leads to restlessness, for the inner and outer persons conflict. By itself, a sense of duty can lead to such external faithfulness, but this is the sort of faithfulness that often fails to motivate us adequately.

If I am faithful to my church in spirit, I enjoy an ongoing romance with my church and each responsibility of the pastorate, driven both by a sense of duty *and* by passion. I need to keep dreaming about what *my* church can become, not envying someone else's church. I need to stir up my love for my people and think about the good in each of them. I need to pray and believe for my congregation. Passion is nothing less than a painstaking discipline of the heart.

Inner faithfulness had to be what made John the Baptist who he was. Imagine how boring the desert could be before he broke onto the public scene! No people to converse with. Not much to read. No entertainment. No visual stimulation. If he had gone into the desert merely out of duty, he would have become a very troubled man. Instead, John was faithful in the center of his soul and thus empowered for every situation.

2. *Work my field to the edges.* I have noticed that farmers find ways to plant seed in every possible square yard of their land. Where there are rocks, they dig them up and haul them away. Where there are trees, they cut them down, pull up the roots, and burn them. Where the land is arid, they irrigate. I have seen farmers in Illinois use earth-moving equipment to improve the lay of the land.

In a similar way, I am trying to work the ministry field God has given me right to the fences, and even in my small church it is a challenging task. I have a list of people I am trying to lead into a committed relationship with Jesus Christ. I also have a list of unchurched people, nominally Christian, who have visited our church but not yet found a church home. I have still another list of people who call our church home—some who attend regularly, others sporadically. I regularly review these lists and attempt to follow the leading of the Holy Spirit about whom to contact through a phone call or letter and how to help them move more fully into the will of God.

I have found ministry becomes boring when I stray

from such hands-on ministry with people, and often I have done that. In my previous churches, I emphasized preaching and the devotional life and only sporadically spent time in one-on-one discipleship or evangelism. As a result, I suffered bouts of restlessness regarding the church. When I remain tucked away in my office, simply writing sermons and shuffling papers, or if I solely challenge others from the pulpit, I can lose touch with the relevance of my ministry to my hearers. But if I stay in the trenches with people, get face-to-face with them and appeal to them to cross the next line of commitment, I am stretched to the limit. In fact, I often feel at a complete loss.

Two recent meetings with a student who is an existentialist have jazzed me. He wants to hear about the plausibility of the Christian faith, and each time we have talked cordially for some two hours. He is not yet convinced but he wants to meet again, and I can hardly wait.

Thirty-five people attend our church on a given Sunday, and with growth I know I will have to cut back somewhat on hands-on work with individuals, but I intend to always do some, for I regard it as essential to a proper frame of mind.

3. Wait actively. After years of frustration, I have concluded that much of spiritual life simply comes down to standing fast, hoping in God and his appointed time. "God . . . acts on behalf of those who wait for him" (Isa. 64:4). If I am going to see God's fullest work in and through my life, I must master this patient art.

The waiting can be either endlessly dull or truly exciting.

Several years ago I took my family to a popular water park at the Wisconsin Dells. The lines at the more exciting sites were often long, but I noticed that, at least the first few times, my sons didn't get bored waiting. They watched the other kids on the ride, assessing the challenge, seeing what fun the others were having, wondering if the ride was more than they could handle. As they neared the front of the line, the expectation had them nearly jumping up and down with excitement.

When I wait for God to act, with confident faith and strong hope, I bounce like a ten-year-old about to go down the big water slide. This is faith-waiting, and it has tremendous energy.

My boys have a much different experience when they sit around the house during summer vacation. When they have no idea what to do and nothing to look forward to, they are bored out of their minds. Likewise, when I lack vision and anticipation, I am listless and depressed.

4. *Love the familiar.* My idea of an ideal vacation is a leisurely mix of travel and hanging around Chicago. On the road I enjoy the stimulation of new sights, people, and activities, but travel from the beginning to the end of my vacation wears me out. By the time I have slept in strange beds and eaten in different restaurants for a few days, I have had enough of the new and long to return home and sleep in my own bed with its familiar depression on my side, listen to my stereo with my beloved

Mozart piano concertos, and cook in my kitchen where I can make pasta just the way I like it with my favorite four-cheese sauce.

What I like in a vacation also holds true in life and in ministry. I am happiest when I know how to enjoy both the fresh and the familiar.

The ability to treasure the familiar is not simply a result of increasing age; it is an attitude. Primarily, it involves recognizing the special benefits of the familiar and consciously appreciating them. One reason I enjoy the familiar is that I know I can trust people and settings that have been proven over time. I value the familiar when my soul needs peace and comfort, stability and roots. Sometimes I simply need what is predictable.

Plenty of familiar things in my current ministry bring me great pleasure. When I sit down at my computer, I get a warm feeling; I have used my word processor for six years and it is second nature to me. I enjoy my train ride to the office, which passes the same gritty cityscape and gorgeous skyline every time. I am learning the unique strengths and idiosyncrasies of the people who have been in our church since I arrived, and they bring a smile to my face. These familiar things are part of the rhythms of my life, and even though I know them well, I regularly discover something new in each of them.

I enjoy the familiar most when it is in counterpoint with what is fresh, so I intentionally vary the mix. Sometimes I walk a different path between the train station and my office, always with an exploring and observant eye. Month to month I intentionally preach different styles of sermons—sometimes topical, sometimes an exposition of a scriptural passage; sometimes a long section, other times merely a verse. There is a way to find variety even in the most routine aspects of life.

5. *Never stop asking why and how.* Frankly, boredom has only occasionally been a problem for me in pastoral ministry, and one reason is that I have an insatiable curiosity about the Lord, the Bible, people, preaching, church life, leadership, organizational behavior, and prayer. In my several-decades pursuit to understand all of this, I seem never to have run out of questions. Why did this sermon work better than that one? What motivates people? How can we reach people who do not know Christ? How can I know God better? Why did Jesus tell the Gentile woman that it is not right to throw the children's bread to the dogs? It seems the more questions I get answers for, the more that are raised.

Questions keep ministry fascinating for me. I write them in my journal and pray them to God. I pull out a legal pad to make notes as I analyze a subject or a Scripture. I read books for clues. I listen to audiotapes to try to learn from others. I think about what I can discover from my own experiences. I absolutely, positively love to learn.

For the last year or so my pursuit has been centered on the subject of recognizing God's leading, or, as some call it, hearing God's voice. I have several pages in my DayTimer on which I record any Scriptures I come across in my devotional reading that shed light on the subject, any questions that puzzle me, or principles that come to mind. Gradually, I feel that I am gaining more understanding on the subject.

Being a lifetime learner does not necessarily mean getting formal graduate degrees. At a minimum, though, it means asking questions and seeking answers. Once we lose our curiosity and wonder, we start to stagnate.

When boredom continues

If despite the above approaches to ministry, I still find myself in a season of boredom and restlessness, I ask myself several questions:

1. Are my spiritual disciplines energized by the Holy Spirit? The diagnosis of any stagnation problem will usually include a recognition of my need for a fresh anointing of the Holy Spirit. Even before I came to Christ, I was a disciplined person—especially in training for sports—and I have found I can bring that natural discipline into my devotional life—usually to positive effect, but sometimes negative. It is possible to engage in "spiritual" disciplines in a way that could be better described as natural disciplines. That is, when I am not truly dependent on the Holy Spirit. I can read so many chapters daily in the Bible, for example, but in an exclusively rationalistic manner that is insensitive to the leading of the Spirit. Or I can pray systematically through a list, or memorize large portions of Scripture—all in my own power.

Discipline has its place but it is not enough. I need grace and a fresh touch from God. As Zechariah 4:6 says,

"'Not by might nor by power, but by my Spirit,' says the Lord Almighty." I have learned—and need to keep learning—to engage in spiritual disciplines with an intentional awareness of the Holy Spirit.

Like Abraham, I need to dig fresh wells in the Promised Land. When I am bored, I can keep planting seeds again and again in a dry field; or I can dig for water or build an irrigation system as I plant the seeds. On a regular basis, I desperately need a fresh anointing.

2. *Have I asked the Lord about the source of my boredom?* As much as I believe in the need to ask God for direction, especially when I am at a loss, my tendency is to avoid doing so. There are several reasons why. To center completely on the Scripture and the Holy Spirit and to wait for an impression from the Lord is time consuming, usually requiring three to six hours, for me. Often I come away from that time with a sense that God has given me his mind; but sometimes not. Even when I do feel that I have his mind, it is a subjective impression that may leave me feeling uncertain.

In any case, when I am at the end of my resources, unless I ask God why it is so, I linger in stagnation. Sooner or later, seeking God leads to a breakthrough.

The procedure that generally helps me is to begin by asking God to impress on my heart a particular place in Scripture to read. Then I wait until I sense some direction or interest. Finally, I read that portion of Scripture, and more often than not the words have life and relevance for me, bringing fresh promise or correction.

3. *Have I slacked off from the hard things of ministry?* I can stagnate in ministry when I have been lazy as a thinker and fallen into a rut. On the other hand, I stay challenged beyond anything I can fully accomplish if I periodically do several things: (a) Evaluate the church and my effectiveness regularly, asking the hard questions about our overall effectiveness and spirituality. (b) Keep sharpening a *strategy* of ministry that bears fruit. (c) Set some goals (though I have mixed feelings about numerical goals). (d) Plan how to solve our problems, reach our goals, and fulfill our vision. (e) Fast and pray for God to inspire this entire process. Hard digging like this leaves me almost unbearably excited about ministry.

There are always a thousand more challenges and opportunities to grow where I am. Normally God wants to give me new vision, not a new address.

4. *Am I neglecting the fundamentals?* Has my love for God cooled? Have I lost my spiritual vitality? Has my love for the people of God waned? Does it matter to me that people without Christ will go to eternal judgment? Do I believe God will answer my prayers? Do I believe God's promises, rightly understood, will be fulfilled in my life sooner or later? Have I lost hope? Am I ready for the return of Christ? Do I love the Gospel message and am I still devoted to sharing the Good News with every person I can in every daily situation possible? Am I living for what is most important in life?

5. *Other assessment questions.* Have I gotten too comfortable? Have I become passive instead of an initiator? Have I stopped attending to growth points in my character? Do I merely want to get out of a situation rather than grow through it? Have I arranged my life to be too safe, in effect clinging to the shallow end of the pool? Have I moved away from the motivations that originally compelled me into ministry and begun to work from ones that cannot rightly sustain me: careerism, professionalism, financial security? Have I neglected significant time spent in seeking the Lord in a *variety* of spiritual disciplines? Am I renewing my vision? Have I considered both the spiritual and natural causes of my stagnation? Am I getting enough input and stimulation?

Busting complacency

That the most challenging and important work imaginable can become boring should tell me something about its cure. Novelist Samuel Butler said, "The man who lets himself be bored is even more contemptible than the bore."

Ouch! As much as I hate to admit it, when boredom strikes, the responsibility is mine. It is not my setting that has become stagnant, I have. Through God's grace, I, too, am fully capable of restoring the passion.

The cycle of growth and stagnation is predictable. The Lord places me in a situation that stretches me. Gradually I grow in dependence upon God, upon knowledge, upon experience—to where I feel comfortable with what I am doing. Then I begin to plateau and stagnate.

At this point I have some options. I can become complacent; I can pursue other interests and be diverted from what God has called me to do; or I can press hard into a new cycle of growth in which I dig deeper and draw closer to the Lord.

On second thought, there is no choice.

12

GOING WITH THE GRAIN

AT TIMES I HAVE FELT AS THOUGH who I really am did not match what I was doing. At one time I worked my way through a phone directory, teeth clenched, telemarketing for unchurched people—enduring something that was the last thing in the world I wanted to do. Such experiences always leave me with a hollow feeling and the sense that I cannot sustain this kind of activity for very long.

In a TV interview I did, I noticed that the bookshelf in the background, like most of the set, was only for show. The "books" were spines with nice-looking titles but no printed pages inside. Sometimes I have felt as though I was propping up a similar pastoral facade. I was doing what I thought had to be done but I was not acting authentically from the core of my being. My outside actions and inside motivations were in conflict.

Sunday night services are an example of what once commonly gave me this feeling. After pouring my heart out on a Sunday morning, I would go home and have lunch and a short nap. By four o'clock I felt lower than any other time of the week. The last thing I wanted to do was stand in front of a crowd, try to smile and be enthusiastic, and get my heart into another sermon. My throat hurt; my legs were tired. I can honestly say that on most Sunday nights for several years, I raised at least one person from the dead! I am basically an introvert, and I felt I had been with people enough for one day.

Of course, most occupations require that people do *some* things they do not feel like doing. Fulfilling such responsibilities doesn't make you a fake; you are simply dealing with the real world. Nevertheless, at times I have had to wonder, *Is God in this? Are my feelings a signal that we should be doing something different? Am I trying to fight Goliath wearing Saul's armor?*

Equally important, such times have made me wonder how long I could sustain what I was doing. To work from something other than the core of who I am draws a tremendous amount of energy, like a locomotive pulling a long freight train up a hill. Consequently, when authenticity is lacking, I perform poorly and often feel like quitting.

The pursuit of authentic ministry is therefore of vital importance. How do I fulfill the demands of my role without losing the sense of who I am as a person? Is it possible in ministry to always feel a true match between who I am and what I do? Can I step outside my comfort zone for Christ and yet feel as though I am working from my core being?

Genuine authenticity

When I think about authenticity, I have to be sure I am working from a biblical concept, not a distorted notion from pop-psychology. I have grown up hearing my culture tell me about the need to find myself, know myself, be true to myself. While valid in many respects, these ideas can slip into error when they leave God out of the picture. God is the ultimate standard of what makes me authentic, not my DNA helix.

I cannot find *authenticity*, though a good word, in any of my Bible versions; rather, Scripture addresses the concept of personal genuineness with words like *sincerity, truth, hypocrisy, faithfulness.* Authenticity suffers a humanistic distortion when the sentiment becomes "I've gotta be me." Although the concept is not necessarily false, the Bible shows much less concern with the notion of whether I am true to myself and endless concern with whether I am true to God's will.

What I find unambiguously clear in Scripture is that my authenticity as a minister stands like a table on four legs:

1. *My spiritual gifts.* God calls me to recognize the spiritual gifts he has given me and to manage them faithfully as my primary responsibility. When I feel hollow, the problem may be that I am minoring in the areas of my spiritual gifts.

2. *God's leading.* God expects me to obey his call whether or not I feel qualified. When God tells me to do something that lies outside my sense of competence, it means one of two things: (a) I may be qualified and not know it. (b) God can make me qualified when the need arises. He told a reluctant Moses, "Who made your mouth?"

One criterion for authenticity is to recognize what God's direction and purpose is for my life, not what I feel natural doing. The point is less *Who am I?* and more *How is God working through me?*

3. *Christian character*. The ultimate standard to which I am to be true is not some subjective notion of my identity, but the person of Christ as reflected in the objective teachings of Scripture. For example: Is shyness a part of my personality, or is it a lack of love for others? Am I introverted, or self-centered? The difference between personality and character can be gray, at best. My ultimate authenticity is based not on the personality formed by my genes and experiences, but rather the character of Christ imparted to me by the Holy Spirit.

4. *Wholehearted obedience*. God calls me to follow his bidding willingly, not reluctantly. If I halfheartedly obey, I will feel—and be—inauthentic. In such moments my lack of genuineness has more to do with my chief desires and less to do with how I am wired. God shows his concern with authentic obedience in 2 Corinthians 9:7: "Each man should give what he has decided in his heart to give, not reluctantly or under compulsion, for God loves a cheerful giver."

If I feel hollow, it may be that I am more excited about other things than I am about the will of God.

Ring-true ministry

After two years in my current position, I regularly marvel at how well this church fits me—and how satisfying such a match is. For the first time, I feel I am working largely from my core being. I love what I do and look forward to office days and Sundays. I feel I could pastor this church for a millennium and beg for more. My responsibilities, however, differ little from those in my previous churches. (We do have Sunday night meetings!) What has changed?

1. *I now minister in a manner truer to my personality.* Generally my temperament is not that of a high-energy cheerleader. Nevertheless, in my early ministry I usually tried to be very enthusiastic. While enthusiasm helps in many ways, mine was sometimes forced.

In the current stage of my life, I am more enthusiastic when emotion flows naturally from some cause; but as a general rule I am not wired for enthusiasm. In terms of the classic four categories of personality, I lean toward the melancholy and choleric rather than the sanguine or phlegmatic. Even when I feel deeply anointed by the Holy Spirit, I am more apt to be quiet than loud. When I force enthusiasm, I sense in others the discomfort of being subjected to what is emotionally contrived, a discomfort similar to what one feels in the presence of a man wearing a cheap toupee.

I forced my enthusiasm in the past partly because I thought others expected it. Last week, for instance, one man who has attended our church for a year told me that on a business trip he visited a church that was having revival services. He described how much he appreciated those meetings. "They were really on fire," he said. He told me he didn't intend his comment as a slam on me or our church, but the implication was clear.

If my spirituality is lacking, I need the challenge of such a comment, but now I am secure enough to express my zeal for God in a manner that is genuine for me (which I would describe as animated rather than loud). I trust love, sincerity, faith, the Holy Spirit, and God's truth to carry the day.

2. *I have a greater sense of freedom.* In my previous settings I felt much more constrained about how we did church. For example, our services had to have a certain level of formality; we needed to have certain programs.

My feeling of obligation arose from several sources. Wisdom had something to do with it, I trust, for change is always risky, especially for an inexperienced pastor. Temperament played a part too. I think as well that I had a commendable desire to lay aside my own preferences for what I thought was the good of others.

It is likely, however, that my sense of constraint did not always benefit me or the church. Although I must not be, nor do I want to be, a self-indulgent leader, I recognize now that what suits me may very well be of the Lord. As one called and filled with the Spirit, I must assume that God inspires many of my passions and sensibilities about how to do church. Therefore, as I die to self in order to serve others, I still may often order ministry in a way that goes with the grain of who I am. I believe God works through the design he has given me.

This freedom to go with my own grain is crucial to authenticity. If I persist in a manner of ministry that feels alien, and probably lacks the Lord's blessing, I will feel hollow.

In my present church I feel an exhilarating sense of freedom to experiment—within the boundaries of wisdom and self-giving love. As never before, I feel I have options. If I prepare people properly, we can try different ideas to see whether God is in them. I am doing a higher proportion of things that I feel passionate about, that I truly believe in, and that I have confidence will be fruitful. The point of this freedom is not to please myself but to find a style of ministry that God works through and that suits me and the church.

For example, we have tried several different ways of praying for people at the end of our church services. I often give traditional "altar calls." I have sometimes broken the congregation into small groups in order that people may pray for one another. I have invited people to come forward for prayer after the service is dismissed. I have asked people to pray silently where they are. We have even tried holding a mini-prayer meeting at the end of the Sunday morning service, inviting everyone to spend ten minutes in prayer. Although I have not yet found an expression for prayer that works ideally in our church, I intend to keep experimenting.

Of course, many things still do not match me perfectly. I wear a suit on Sunday mornings, even though I am the only one to do so in our church and I feel out of place. I suggest that others call me "Pastor" or "Pastor Brian," even though I would be more comfortable without the title. I freely choose to deny myself these prefer-ences, though, for the sake of what I feel is best for others.

3. *I focus on how everything can serve my highest goals.* I feel as though my ministry has a solid core when my activities align with my purposes and goals—even if those ministry activities fall outside my strengths. If I feel hollow about my work, I may have missed the con-nection between how it can or already does serve the goals I am deeply motivated about.

For instance, administrative paper work, in itself, leaves me cold. In the past I completed my monthly financial report to my denominational superiors with a sense of frustration. Now I remind myself that my paper work fulfills a purpose I feel strongly about: the oversight of my church's corporate health. Our finances are obvi-ously of one cloth with that. We must have financial integrity and we must make wise, vision-based expendi-tures over the long run if we are to accomplish our mis-sion. To do that I must be involved. When I think in these terms, I am working from the core of my soul.

To work from my core, I need to know what my high-est purposes are and then see how what I do serves those purposes. If a particular task does not do this, I must find a way to give that work to someone else whenever possible.

Pushing the envelope

In Scripture, the Lord often called people to serve in ways outside their comfort zone, whether it was washing feet or walking on water. When the Lord calls me to do this, I need to be able to expand the envelope of my service with a sense of authenticity in order to persevere. This works if I attend to three things.

1. *Discover the genuineness of God's grace in me.* The familiar passage in 2 Corinthians 12, in which Paul says God's power is expressed most fully in our weaknesses, teaches me a critical lesson: God's grace is one authenticating element in my life. Who am I and what is genuine to me? The answer includes not only my personality but also whatever God adds to me by his Spirit. His power in me is also who I am.

No matter what I do, as I rely upon his grace, I experience a deep reality to my ministry, for I fellowship with my Creator, who is the Truth. As I serve with a greater dependence on the Holy Spirit, my experience deepens with the One in whom I live and move and have my being. What could be more authentic than that? My genuineness at this point is not necessarily a combination of my ministry and my core self but that of my ministry and the Core of the Universe—in me!

For example, while cold-contact outreach has at times sapped my resources because "sales" would be my last choice for an occupation, at other times outreach has exhilarated and satisfied me immensely. I think this is true because I have had to pray much and rely completely on God's help at these times, and I have seen him work through me.

2. *Wholeheartedly seek God's will as my highest purpose.* My core self comprises not merely my personality and my abilities but also my values and purpose. In other words, my core being includes whatever makes me tick: all my motivations. Thus an integrating sense of genuineness comes from my decision to serve God in any way he desires—not merely in a preferred role such as preaching. My main goal in life is not to preach but to serve God. Preaching is a legitimate subsidiary purpose.

When I left pastoral ministry for three years to work full time with an editorial staff, it was a hard decision because I had not lost my love of pastoral ministry and, frankly, I disliked the prospect of sitting in front of a computer every day. I made the move, however, because I felt God had clearly led me to do so, and that was what mattered most to me. My life purpose gave authenticity to a task that was not my first order of calling. Sometimes other pastors would ask if it was hard "to leave the ministry." If I had truly left the ministry, I would have been heartbroken, but I had not. I simply ministered in a different capacity, one in which God wanted me to serve, and that is what I want above all else in my life.

3. *Honestly acknowledge my personal inability and fallenness without God.* Deluding myself about my abilities or character is the quickest way to become a fake. Facing hard reality puts me on genuine ground.

For instance, I have faced the fact that I will never build a church through leadership charisma. I just don't have it. If I believed I did, I would feel every day like the king who had no clothes. Further, I have confessed character weaknesses such as my inclination toward despair. As a result, when I step outside my comfort zone, I may battle despair and I may struggle with the limitations of my personality, but I do not feel like a hypocrite or a phony because I know God intends to use me in spite of these encumbrances.

I am not pulling anything over on myself or others. I acknowledge that I am genuinely unable to minister without God's help. As Paul said, "Not that we are competent in ourselves to claim anything for ourselves, but our competence comes from God" (2 Cor. 3:5).

Authentic ministry resembles a good jump-shot in basketball. Sports announcers occasionally comment on the excellent technique of a good shooter. The player does not merely flip the ball toward the basket or shoot across his body in a contorted fashion. Instead, he squares his shoulders to the basket, jumps well, and with each shot has an identical stroke. All his motions integrate to support the shot, meaning that his whole body shoots, not only his hands.

When I minister genuinely, everything within me supports the effort. When I minister from my core self, I do so with strength and greater effectiveness. When I am authentic, I can stand and stay with a sense of stability and integrity. I become a person of truth through whom the God of truth can flow.

Only when I am authentic can I persevere with spiritual vitality—strong to the finish.